D0341497

A LETTER TO MY FATHER

/ / / / /

Helen Madamba Mossman

/ / / / /

A LETTER TO MY FATHER
Growing Up Filipina and American

/ / / / /

Helen Madamba Mossman

UNIVERSITY OF OKLAHOMA PRESS : NORMAN

Library of Congress Cataloging-in-Publication Data

Mossman, Helen Madamba, 1933–
    A letter to my father : growing up Filipina and American / Helen Madamba Mossman.
    p.   cm.
    ISBN 978-0-8061-3909-8 (hardcover: alk. paper)
    1. Mossman, Helen Madamba, 1933– 2. Arzaga Madamba, Jorge, d. 1963. 3. World
War, 1939–1945—Personal narratives, Philippine. 4. World War, 1939–1945—Philippines. 5. Teenage girls—Philippines—Biography. 6. Filipino Americans—Biography.
7. Journalists—United States—Biography.   I. Title.

    D811.5.M675 2008
    940.53'599092—dc22
    [B]

                                                                        2007021248

The paper in this book meets the guidelines for permanence and durability of the
Committee on Production Guidelines for Book Longevity of the Council on Library
Resources. ∞

1 2 3 4 5 6 7 8 9 10

To my brother, my friend, Dr. Jorge J. Madamba

and

to my children, Dan, Sara, Kevin, and Jayne,
who have given meaning to my life;

in memory of their grandparents
Jorge and Iva Madamba

and to Bill and Jack Harrison,
who fought in the Pacific to rescue their Aunt Johnny

Psalm 78: 14–16

He led them with a cloud by day,
and all the night through with a glow of fire.

He split the hard rocks in the wilderness
and gave them drink as from the great deep.

He brought streams out of the cliffs,
and the waters gushed out like rivers.

Contents

/ / /

Contents

Illustrations

/ / /

Photographs

Maps

Preface and Acknowledgments
/ / /

I began this book when I was in the seventh grade in Woodward, Oklahoma. Frances Lawrence, editor and publisher of the *Woodward Daily Press*, asked me to write a series of articles describing my family's life in the Philippines during World War II. The articles were published in the *Daily Press* in the summer of 1946. Five or six years later, while I was in college at Oklahoma A&M, I wrote a couple of short stories based on those experiences for assignments in a creative writing course. Over five decades, I've written reflections of the events of my early childhood, intending to turn them into a book someday.

I was thirty years old before I finally came to terms with who I am and what my true convictions are. During the decade of the sixties, I read news stories and watched on television the struggle for civil rights and the awfulness of the Vietnam War. I became an activist in the women's movement because

I couldn't stand by, complacently living what I'd sought as the All-American dream. In 1973 I was a single mother raising four young children, and I had to call on the resilience and determination my father and mother had demonstrated during World War II. When I was fifty I began an exhilarating and sometimes hair-raising career as a journalist.

It pleases me that I've finally finished writing *A Letter to My Father*. It tells of the gift his life was, not just to me but to unnamed others who benefited from his knowledge, his intelligence, and his dedication to all humanity.

The characters in *Letter* are as close to their original personae as I can remember. A few minor characters are composites of persons I observed as a child or who were described to me by my parents and other family members and friends. Many of the episodes are compressed because I can't elaborate on details that happened so long ago. I see myself as a storyteller of events as they took place when I was a little girl eight to twelve years old.

I want to express my gratitude to my friends and family who drove me to finish this book. It was sixty years in the writing, but many people in my life refused to let me rest until it was complete. I thank my daughter Sara Seeman, who held my hand and kept my fingers on the computer during the last days; my cousins Betsy Harrison and Laine Massey, who never stopped reminding me of my obligation to our grandchildren to tell this story; to my brother, Dr. Jorge J. Madamba, who knew I would somehow get it all together and get it written.

I am grateful to my husband, Romain Mossman, who for thirty years of marriage has been compassionate and patient with my career as a journalist. Without his support and understanding, I would never have been able to fulfill my professional ambitions as managing editor of a daily newspaper, beat reporter, columnist, and author.

I would also like to thank Matthew Bokovoy and Alice Stanton of the University of Oklahoma Press for their unfailing encouragement and publishing expertise, and Jay Fultz, a superb copy editor and fellow writer.

And finally, my thanks to Rob Roberson, director of the Plains Indians and Pioneers Museum in Woodward, and to the museum staff for their indispensable technical help and professional interest in this project.

A LETTER TO MY FATHER

/ / / / /

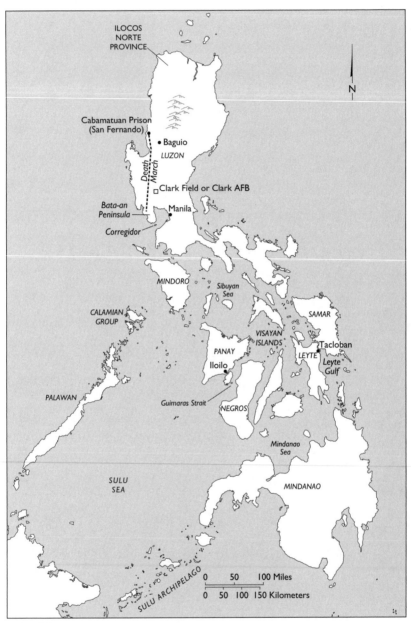

The Philippines

Introduction
My Father,
Jorge Arzaga Madamba
/ / /

My father is more real to me now than he has been at any time since I was twelve years old. Although he died more than forty years ago, he is a presence I recognize after nearly a lifetime of locking him away behind an emotional door down a long-forgotten hallway of my mind. It is the same heavy door that closed off the Visayan language we once shared, a language I have not spoken for more than half a century.

Visayan was the language I learned simultaneously with English, because I am biracial. My father was a Filipino and my mother an American. I was born in the Philippines in 1933 and lived there until I was twelve years old. My younger brother (my only sibling) and I had never been to the United States until 1945. We spent World War II in hiding from the Japanese on the island of Negros.

My memories of my dad are like pictures pasted in a neglected photo album—static, incomplete, hard to place in time. I try now to remember how he looked, the expressions on his face, the sound of his voice, the way he spoke, the things he said. There are so few remnants of him from my childhood.

I always think of my father when I hear the voice of a non-native speaker of English struggling to communicate in American idiom. The awkward, halting syntax, the mangled grammar and pronunciation, the stilted vocabulary, the accent that baffled many of his monolingual English-speaking listeners—they all conjure up his presence. I studied linguistics in graduate school because I was fascinated with language as I heard it from him when I was growing up. Remembering a few of his linguistic blunders now warms my heart. For instance, he would ask someone to "broom" the floor when it was dirty. He had trouble with gender pronouns: "He is my sister." Prepositions were never quite right, no matter how hard he tried: "Thank you of calling." When I was a teenager, I wanted to run and hide when he was conversing with someone American; God forbid if that person was a classmate or my high school idol.

At least one of my father's characteristics was passed on to me, for which I will always be proud. He was never intimidated by class or social position or economic status. He had friends who were corporate titans, U.S. senators, and celebrities in the arts. Yet he often sat on the ground with peasants who loved to exchange stories with him. He was a gracious host and a good-natured guest, and could strike up a pleasant—and interesting—conversation with anyone he met on the street, in an airliner, or at the post office. After the war, when he worked overseas with the United Nations Relief and Rehabilitation Administration and then Point Four and USAID (the Agency for International Development), he quickly learned to get along in the local language or dialect of every place in which he was posted. However, I chuckle now at the thought that, if Dad spoke those various tongues as badly as he spoke English, it was his charm and warm personality more than language mastery that won him so many friends over the globe.

Because of what he did as a soldier and a citizen, as a husband, a father, the head of a family during World War II—and before as well as after—I salute him as a hero. He was a courageous man in an era when courage was recognized and appreciated, not used for political bombast. Dad liked to talk about our wartime ordeal, but for me it was an embarrassment because it called attention to the fact that I wasn't as all-American and all-Oklahoman as I tried to pretend.

Now I tell my friends proudly that my dad fought in the war and that he saved not only the lives of his fellow soldiers and civilian countrymen but also my life and the lives of my mother and my little brother. Literally. Directly. We too were in the combat zone and Japanese soldiers marched through the jungle and across the mountains of an island in the Philippines, hunting us down to shoot us dead if they could not capture us and take us into their encampments as trophies. In my early adolescent mind after 1945, my father's bravery was secondary to my desperate need to blend, to be accepted by my peers in America, not to be singled out because of my nationality, my physical appearance, my incredibly "different" previous life. And, most of all, not to be something other than American, white American. I wanted to be conventional but I had to be more than average, an over-achiever to prove that I was not someone of an "inferior" race.

So it was that after I came to the United States with my father and my mother and my nine-year-old brother in 1945, exactly a month after my twelfth birthday, I repudiated the life I had lived from my birth in the Philippines. Today I can barely remember what it was to be a Filipina, because in my mind I never was. Despite my long black braided hair, my dark brown eyes, my slender build, my olive skin, and for a time, my sibilant accent, I was determined to be the American that my mother was.

I abandoned my father emotionally when the war ended. He was no longer part of my life. Although he was present in our American household while he recovered his health and earned a master's degree at Oklahoma

A&M College, my father never again during his lifetime received my filial love, respect, and honor.

Jorge Madamba was from another culture, another era, another way of life. He died in 1963 and I look back now and realize how much I missed. Although I never said these words to him when he was living, I shall say them now.

I must have known that you were brave. Bravery was something people understood in the 1940s. You did not, like some of your countrymen, calculate the odds of survival and submit to an enemy army when all hope was gone after the defeat of American forces in the Philippines by Japan in 1942. You refused to surrender yourself, your country, or your family to the Japanese invaders. Your wife was an American and your children were half-American. Your pride as a Filipino prevented you from giving in to a foreign government that had no respect for your country's sovereignty or its people's right to self-determination.

When you risked your life on jungle trails, in mountain ridges and ravines, and lowland irrigation ditches, in bodegas that stored food and ammunition, in open rice fields where there was no place to hide, in fragile little outriggers on the Sulu Sea, it was out of devotion to the eventual establishment of democracy and independence in the Philippines. And you would not betray the flag of the United States, the country where you earned a college education, where you were trained to be a soldier, where you became an officer in the United States Army. Your allegiance to the country where your wife was born and would forever be a patriot never wavered because, in your mind, your children would live in the United States and be educated there. The four of us knew, without a doubt, that we would live in the United States after the war.

From the last week of 1941 until mid-1945, you led an army, a guerrilla army of farmers and boys, some of whom were barely in their teens. In that army there were also women who were mothers, grandmothers, housewives, shopkeepers, teachers, and tailors. You led them to fight for the survival of your children and their children to the next day, the next year, to adulthood and, for some of us, to the next millennium.

Your wife was self-sufficient, hard-working, strong-minded. Like many women who grew up to vote in the 1920s, she challenged convention, being determined to control her own destiny—and she wanted to know more of the world beyond the borders of Oklahoma.

Somewhere in my growing up, Dad, I left you. In a family scrapbook there is a snapshot taken just a month before you died. You and I are sitting on a sofa in the living room of the Tulsa, Oklahoma, home you and Mother built for your retirement. Two of my children are in your arms. I am sitting at the other end of the sofa, as far away from you as I can get. My arms are crossed stiffly on my lap and my whole body is in closed position. I was your alien daughter, having nothing to do with you, wanting no part of who you were, or what you were to me.

I have at last formed a posthumous perception of you. You were loved and adulated by many but not by me. I was self-absorbed and determined to be a white Anglo-Saxon Protestant American.

And so I want to tell your story because now I recognize that none of the goals I have reached, none of the good life I have lived, would have happened had you not been my father.

1

A Handsome Young Stranger

/ / /

My father was born on April 23, 1898, in a small town in the province of Ilocos Norte at the far end of Luzon, south across an ocean strait from Taiwan. He was the second child of a landowner farmer. His mother, Antonia (*née* Arzaga) Madamba, died when Dad was a baby. His father, Julian Madamba, married again and six more children were born into the Madamba family.

Adela, my father's elder sister, was his surrogate mother. After he finished high school, he worked his way to the United States, and Aunt Adela sent him money, a few pesos each month, to help him while he attended Oklahoma A&M College.

I believe Jorge Madamba landed in Vancouver, British Columbia, in 1920. From there he made his way to Oklahoma, working as a dishwasher along the way to pay for train fare. I never heard the story of his travel from him. What I remember were the tales of his youth my mother told when I was a child.

Oklahoma A&M College in Stillwater was a leader among American land-grant colleges that opened their doors to foreign students, particularly students who were interested in learning about modern agriculture. My father was influenced to go to college in the United States by a teacher from Oklahoma who was working in the Philippines, perhaps a missionary who taught agricultural science in my father's high school.

Dad was a small man. He stood 5 feet 6 inches in his prime and never weighed much more than 140 pounds. His black hair was beginning to gray even in his twenties, and by the time he was thirty-five or forty, it was turning white. Out of vanity, he used hair dye, which made him look like a young boy in pictures of those days. After World War II, my father's hair was silver.

There were other Asians on the campus of Oklahoma A&M College in the '20s. My dad and four or five fellow countrymen stuck together and supported each other through what must have been some fearful and lonely times. Because he was slight of stature and singularly unfamiliar with heavy machinery, Jorge couldn't get hired to work in construction or outside maintenance, campus jobs that were generally available to male students. He possessed a skill, however, that few other men had—he could use a typewriter. Not many office administrators thought to ask a man about his clerical skills.

The college housing office was managed by Miss Edith Prosser. "Your room and board will come to $25 a month," she said when my father came to her for help in finding a place to live. "I know a boarding house that's run by a widow woman and she only takes boys. She has three boys of her own and a daughter. Her basement can house three boarders and, right now, it's vacant."

My father lowered his head. He simply didn't have $25 a month to pay for living expenses. At best, Adela's monthly money order was for no more than $5 and he hadn't had any luck finding employment that paid enough to cover such rent.

Miss Prosser's voice was firm. "I really don't have anything for less than that," she said. "Is there anything at all you can do to earn the money?"

Taking a deep breath, my dad said, "Maybe I work here. I broom floor, remove dust from furniture, take out wastebaskets? I help you for anything you need."

Miss Prosser looked around her cubbyhole office. Yes, it did need some cleaning and she hadn't had time to see to that. Janitorial service was not provided by the university. Female employees, at least, were expected to do their own housekeeping.

"I can't pay you a lot," Miss Prosser said. "But if you want to make $10 a month, I'll see that you get that. You can probably clean some other offices and my colleagues and I will split your wages."

My father was ecstatic. He took the rental agreement form for Mrs. Rogers' basement and proceeded to 230 North Duncan Street to meet his potential landlady.

On the way, he stopped by Swim's Campus Corner drug store and lunch counter, where he had previously applied for work. He told the proprietor that he had a lead on a permanent address if he could make a few more dollars to cover the rent. Given that Jorge had demonstrated ambition and perseverance, Mr. Swim reconsidered his first decision not to hire any more students. He gave my father a weekend position as a dishwasher, for which he would be paid a dollar a day and the day's meals.

When he met with Mrs. Rogers, Jorge negotiated the rent to a lower amount by signing on to wash all the windows of the house and maintain the yard. Also, he pointed out that since he would be eating at Swim's on Saturday, she could deduct that expense from her day's groceries. As an added persuasion, he told Mrs. Rogers about two friends, Filipinos, who were also looking for rooms. If all three rented from her, she agreed to reduce the monthly rent further by a few dollars.

Mrs. Rogers' garden was his joy. During the Oklahoma growing season, Jorge tended hollyhocks, honeysuckle vines, and okra plants, none of which he'd ever known in his home country although most of the other vegetables and flowers were familiar to him. The pleasure of cultivating growing things was no different in the United States than in the Philippines, where, as a boy, he planted rice and harvested coconuts, picked bananas, and cut sugar cane. The feel of the earth and the thrill of seeing seedlings sprout up filled the hole of homesickness in his heart.

Mrs. Rogers was delighted with the arrangement. Her three sons had little interest in yard work, although at least one of them became an internationally known agriculturalist. The Rogers brothers, instead, were immersed in the sport of wrestling and the prospect of competing in the 1928 Olympics.

For Jorge, learning to speak English well enough to keep up his studies and staying ahead of his always meager financial condition were full-time distractions. But a few weeks after he started janitoring in Miss Prosser's college housing office, he asked her permission to use the typewriter to compose a letter to his sister.

"Sure, anytime you need it, if it's after hours," said Miss Prosser.

It was a few minutes after the office's closing time. Jorge inserted a sheet of paper into the machine and began to type. The speed of the keys striking the platen astounded Miss Prosser, who had never seen a man operate a typewriter so competently. Years later, she described the rat-a-tat-tat of his typing as "sounding like a machine-gun." Looking over the young man's shoulder, Miss Prosser was annoyed because she couldn't read the letter, which was written in Ilocano.

Jorge's competence on the typewriter earned him a quick promotion to office work and a small increase in salary. In the office hierarchy he became the lead man—actually he was the only man in the typing pool— who kept up with every deadline and knew what was in every file.

2

Iva Harrison

/ / /

My father and mother's love story began in a summer of the early 1920s. There were not many students on the Oklahoma A&M campus between June and September and the days were long and languid.

Iva Harrison was a teacher. Her winters were spent in one-room school-houses in Woodward and Ellis counties in northwest Oklahoma. She started teaching when she was nineteen, just out of Fort Supply High School. Although she could have continued that occupation until she married, Iva Harrison had a broader plan for her future. She wanted a college degree, so she enrolled in summer sessions at Oklahoma A&M College. She knew the road ahead to her destination was going to be long—at the earliest, it would take her six or eight summer sessions to graduate. But Iva Harrison was a diligent and brilliant student who excelled in every class she took. When she received her bachelor of science diploma with a major in home economics in 1931, she was in the top five percent of her graduating class and a member of Phi Kappa Phi, the land-grant college equivalent of Phi Beta Kappa.

Jorge Madamba and Iva Harrison met on a campus tennis court. Both were highly competitive, and while Iva had the advantage in height, Jorge was quicker and more agile. They stopped playing against each other and formed a doubles team that vanquished most of their opponents.

The summer sessions were halcyon days of picnics and church socials, watermelon feasts, and hikes through the Payne County hills. When fall came, Iva went back to northwest Oklahoma to teach another school-house-full of youngsters and Jorge continued his determined slog toward an A&M degree in agronomy.

On July 21, 1927, after my father graduated, he and my mother drove to the Dewey County Courthouse in Taloga, Oklahoma, and were married by a county judge. No family member or friend was at the wedding and I'm not sure her parents knew ahead of time that it was taking place. Mama wore a white silk street-length dress, embroidered on the bodice with pink and blue flowers. She had made her wedding dress at home.

Fifteen years later, my mother's wedding dress burned in the conflagration of World War II.

My father returned to the Philippines within weeks after he and Mother were married. The following September, she returned to college full-time so she could hasten the day when she could join him. Dad had a job with Montilla Sugar Company in Negros Occidental, and he sent Iva money to help her complete her degree. Mother worked summers and then for a full year after graduation, at Boehm's Grocery and Meat Market in Woodward. She saved every penny—as only she could—for the steamship ticket to the Philippines. She arrived in Manila in 1932, and a year later I was born.

From 1942 to 1945, I listened to my mother's oral history of her family in northwest Oklahoma. It was an epic poem, a dramatic saga that brought to life the story of her beginnings.

Mother was born in Kansas in the town of Beagle, a small community south of Osawatomie. Her parents, Silas and Denie Harrison, took their seven children to Oklahoma Territory on the railroad train. Iva, my mother, was the youngest of the Harrison children; she was two years old when the family settled in Ellis County, about twenty miles from Woodward. The year was 1903, four years before statehood.

My cousins and I have different notions about how our grandparents acquired their 160-acre Ellis County claim. My mother's version, which she told to me, was that my Grandfather Harrison homesteaded the land for five years to "prove it up." However a land patent filed in the Ellis County Courthouse in Arnett shows that Silas Harrison received a deed to the land in 1912, five years after Oklahoma became a state and nine years after the family came to Oklahoma. (Denie Harrison's name was not on the deed. For all her hard work, she was not entitled to co-ownership of the land.)

I am guessing at other possibilities. Perhaps Silas and Denie purchased the claim rights from the person who staked it originally in the Cherokee Territory Run of 1893. A goodly number of the first settlers made the Run for investment purposes, and after they had established provisional ownership of the quarter-section claim, they sold it to a latecomer like my grandfather. Or perhaps no one even staked the sagebrush-ridden, canyon-pocked piece of prairie earth. It may still have been available for homesteading ten years after the Run.

Who would have known, more than a century ago, that cattle could thrive on those arid plains and that in good years wheat would bring enough cash to sustain the heirs of sodbusters through another season? And then after the calamity of the Dust Bowl, when the children of so many homesteaders fled to the green promises of California, who would have guessed the bounty of black gold, the oilfields beneath the surface of those parched, brown godforsaken miles of dry unforgiving earth?

My grandparents Harrison and their seven children lived in a sod house my grandfather built with the help of his thirteen-year-old son Marshall. The two of them drove a team of mules and a wagon to the nearest river and cut the timbers for its framework, hauling them back some forty miles to their homesite in Ellis County.

There were three rooms in the sod house—two sleeping rooms and a kitchen-family room. The laundry, bathing, and toilet facilities were outside. Given the imperious nature of Oklahoma winters, it is hard to imagine how the Harrisons always seemed so neat and clean.

The oldest daughters, my aunts Alcie, Frances, and Margaret, were in their teens or older when they came to Oklahoma. Before long, they struck out on their own as teachers in the one-room schools of the northwest Oklahoma territory. Alcie, the eldest, married Roy Hollingsworth and the two of them emigrated to New Mexico Territory, where they homesteaded in the rural area near Springer. Frances married an Ellis County man, J. A. Allen, and lived on a family farm until she died of breast cancer in 1939. Margaret went to New Mexico on her own, staked a claim by herself, and then married her neighbor homesteader, Jess Garlock, who happened to have come from a family that also lived in northwest Oklahoma.

My mother told us of her mother, who always set a Sunday dinner table with a starched white linen tablecloth in a home made of earth and tree trunks and the grassroots of the prairie. The bounty of the land was not nearly as lush and free as what I know today, but it was sturdy and abundant. Hours of summer canning and preserving were required to make its produce last through the winter.

The Harrisons milked Jersey cows and worked with great Percheron horses and giant mules. They raised massive Poland China pigs and Rhode

Island Red chickens. They planted a garden overrunning with green beans and potatoes, tomatoes and turnips, beets and corn. There were wheat fields and hay fields and broomcorn fields, cultivated by walking plow and harvested with a primitive mule-drawn combine. In my grandmother's orchard there were apples and peaches, apricots and pears, currants and various berries.

Although my grandparent's farm sounded like Eden, in truth of course, it was not. Mother also told us about the snowstorms, sandstorms, thunderstorms, and tornadoes that ripped up and paralyzed the little homesteads, and about the searing summer heat and fall drought when nothing could grow in the unbearable sun and the dry red soil, and about the prairie fires that spread, uncontrollable, through the vulnerable little settlements.

Above all else, my mother told about her people, their names, their birthdays and ages, described their temperaments and physical appearance, how they talked and what they liked to do. Though halfway around the world, I knew my cousins, my aunts and uncles, my grandparents, and all their related family connections, as well as the neighbors throughout the county, better than if I were living just down the road.

There was the German family whose claim was across the section line. The parents and children were a sturdy, hardworking lot, said my mother, but they frequently went to community get-togethers, where men and women actually danced, touching, in each other's arms and not necessarily in the arms of their spouses. That scandalized my strait laced grandparents.

In the next section over, there was a family of motherless boys who were tall and gaunt, whose father exerted little parental control. Their farm machinery was left outside to rust in the snow and rain. They didn't take care of their animals. As a result, said my mother, the family was desperately poor. The boys stayed up late at night, reading, wasting coal oil in their reading lamps. No one in the household was awake before daylight, said my mother. Their laziness was an object lesson—the neighbor family was impoverished through their own negligence.

And there were the Grunewalds, the Goodwins, the Burgesses, the Lattas, the Hursts, the Alexanders and the Calhoons and the Pittmans—dozens and dozens of Pittmans, children and grandchildren of my great uncle Henry Pittman, my grandmother's brother, who virtually populated Ellis County.

"I came from honest, hardworking stock," my mother said whenever she began another chapter in her oral history. "We were not poor because we saved. We never went hungry and we never went to bed cold. We were healthy because we got lots of exercise and my sisters and I did farm work like men because we only had one brother."

When my uncle Marshall joined the American Expeditionary Force and went to France to fight in 1918, Mother and her sister Maude stayed out of school to help their father plant and bring in the crops. The two of them later finished high school in Fort Supply where they lived with the Burgess family during the week and did "light housekeeping" to pay for their room and board. I used to think that term meant keeping a lighthouse and I wondered why there would be a lighthouse in the middle of the plains.

My mother had wonderful adventures as a child on the prairie. There was the time she went missing for several hours and her parents asked the neighbors to form a search party to look for her. They scoured the wild countryside and after sundown they called her name, "Iva! Iva! Iva!" (Some of them shouted, without effect, "Ivy! Ivy! Ivy!") Eventually, she was found, not in the bottom of a canyon mauled by coyotes but under the feather bed in her father and mother's sleeping room, where she hid to avoid some chore and had fallen sound asleep. Although the searchers were relieved and probably amused, my grandparents were not pleased and my mother undoubtedly was made to suffer the consequences.

When she was seven years old, Mother fell out of a wagon, and the iron wagon wheels rolled over her left arm and leg, fracturing several bones. The only doctor in the county—Dr. Irwin—was called and he straightened the fractures (without surgery and without anesthetic) by placing weights on the limbs to keep them in line. For several weeks, the little girl lay rigid until the bones knitted together. She recovered to become an athlete, a dynamo who could outwork many men, and an indomitable woman.

My mother loved to tell us about her high school days, especially the year she was recruited to play basketball for a school nearly a hundred miles away. Iva Harrison was five feet ten inches tall, in those days a woman of exceptional height. She was also strong, and had excellent reflexes, just the sort of physical structure that it took to dominate a basketball court.

The Fort Supply High School basketball coach, who incidentally was also the school's superintendent, had taken a better job in Beaver, an up-and-coming community in the Oklahoma Panhandle where school and especially school sports were taken seriously. When he took the Beaver job, the coach started thinking about his team. Of course, his first thoughts were about how to keep the Harrison girls playing for him—and so he offered Iva and Maude Harrison the opportunity to attend Beaver High School, play basketball and live with his family, rent-free. It was an offer they couldn't refuse.

A few years ago the *New York Times* ran a feature story about the evolution of women athletes' game clothing. Included in the accompanying illustrations was a picture of my mother, my Aunt Maude, and their 1917 Beaver High School basketball team. The players wore "middy" blouses, mid-calf length divided skirts, and high-top basketball shoes. If they were uncomfortable, it didn't show. The young women were all smiling in the picture—proud progenitors of today's Title IX beneficiaries.

I never saw either of my grandparents Harrison. They died in the late 1930s when my mother was half a world away. But I see them now in my mind's eye as towering pillars of strength, rigid, immutable, moral as granite, and incapable of doing wrong.

3

Rumors of War

/ / /

While my mother stayed in Oklahoma to finish her degree in home economics at Oklahoma A&M College, my father went home to the Philippines and found a good job with Montilla Sugar Corporation in Negros Occidental. His training as a crops scientist landed him a middle-management position in a large sugar-growing and refining company. Although his classes at A&M probably dealt with little about the production of sugar, Dad nonetheless knew what there was to know about growing cane and converting it into a highly marketable commodity.

As a married woman, Iva Harrison Madamba was no longer employable as a teacher in a rural school. This was, after all, the early '30s in northwest Oklahoma. Not only was her marital status a deterrent to her professional eligibility, the fact that she was the wife of a foreigner might have been a drawback. She had planned to attend graduate school to become a registered dietician because her first love, academically, was the science of foods, but she canceled that ambition to take a job for a year as a clerk-cashier-meat cutter in a Woodward grocery store and butcher shop to earn the money for a steamship ticket to the Philippines.

My grandparents, Silas and Denie Harrison, had retired from their Ellis County farm and moved to town, so my mother lived with them while she worked in Boehm's Grocery on Main Street. Iva faithfully paid for her room and board and did much of the housework. She saved most of her salary to buy her ticket to cross the ocean and rejoin her husband. By the next year, 1932, she had saved enough to make the 8,000-mile trip across the Pacific.

My mother sailed to Manila on the SS *President Wilson*. She kept a journal of her travels, which has long since disappeared, but which I read avidly in my childhood. By train, she went to San Francisco, where she stayed in the St. Francis Hotel. In those days there was no Golden Gate Bridge but she spent a day or so sightseeing alone around the Bay. It was a thrilling experience for a young woman who had never before seen an ocean, or for that matter, a city built on such steep streets. To her, Telegraph Hill must have seemed a mountain.

The voyage on the Dollar Lines ocean liner took her to Hawaii, where she was greeted in Honolulu with a lei and the traditional choral welcome, "Aloha Oe," which she remembered well enough to teach me to sing when I was three. From there, the *President Wilson* sailed to Tokyo, Shanghai, and Hong Kong. In each city Iva Harrison Madamba of Ellis County, Oklahoma, joyously experienced cultures and scenery that she had never dreamed of in Oklahoma or at Oklahoma A&M College.

When she landed in Manila, my mother was greeted by my father and a whole array of relatives. She was formally presented to her father-in-law, Julian Madamba, and her husband's stepmother. Additionally, there were numerous half-brothers, half-sisters, in-laws, cousins, nephews and nieces, endless uncles and aunts, and her indomitable sister-in-law Adela. Iva

Harrison came from a large extended northwest Oklahoma family herself, but the Madambas overwhelmed her.

After a lengthy visit in Luzon with kinfolk, Jorge and Iva boarded an interisland steamer and proceeded to their home in Negros, some 300 miles away by sea.

I was born on August 2, 1933, in the *sitio* of Tinongan, a tiny company town near Isabela, Negros Occidental province. I was delivered by a registered nurse-midwife, Mrs. Seles, who was my mother's first close friend in the Philippines. My mother has told me I had an inordinately large head and in that time neither epesiotomy nor Caesarian section was used in home births, so my arrival was a painful and terrifying ordeal for her. However my mother thrived, and so did I. My father doted on me. In those days it was acceptable for a man to want his first child to be a son, so my parents dressed me in sailor suits and, when I was big enough to walk, Dad and I took a stroll together every evening through "the Central," which is what we called the sugar refinery.

Because of his position in junior management, my father was expected to participate in certain social duties. Iva Harrison had never given a formal dinner party and only rarely attended one, and the expectation that she entertain with a sit-down banquet for twenty-four gave her the vapors. Shortly after she arrived in the Philippines and perhaps while she was suffering the pangs of early pregnancy, it was time for her to reciprocate the many invitations she and my father had received to welcome her into the community. On top of her shyness as a northwest Oklahoma farm girl, my mother was sensitive to the judgments of the women whose husbands worked with my father.

As to whether my mother was able to carry off her role as a gracious hostess, I have no doubt that she did, especially with my father's inestimable way of charming anyone invited to his home. To be sure, the agonizingly long evenings of social small talk and gossip and one-upsmanship concerning

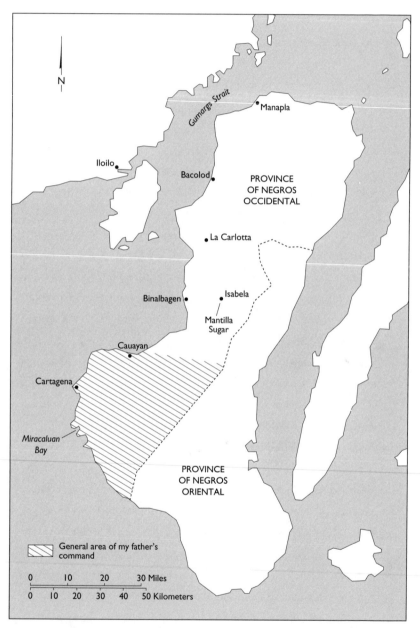

N

Gumargs Strait

Manapla

Iloilo

Bacolod

PROVINCE
OF NEGROS
OCCIDENTAL

La Carlotta

Binalbagen

Isabela

Mantilla
Sugar

Cauayan

Cartagena

Miracaluan
Bay

PROVINCE
OF NEGROS
ORIENTAL

General area of my father's
command

0   10   20   30 Miles

0   10   20   30   40   50 Kilometers

Province of Negros

food, table décor, and servant behavior grated on her nerves to the point that she never again, after the first years in the Philippines, tried or desired to compete with anyone else's idea of social status.

My brother, Jorge Judy, was born two and a half years after me, on January 26, 1936. His middle name was based on my Grandfather Madamba's name, Julian. As a token of respect in both Filipino and American families, parents sometimes felt compelled to name the first son after one of the grandparents, but our parents didn't particularly like the name "Julian." My mother had known a family in Woodward whose last name was Judy, so she thought it would make an appropriate alternative. In later years, Mother said she'd never heard of a girl named "Judy" so she had no idea what ribbing my brother would endure throughout his growing up. I've not called my brother Jorge Judy since he was a child, but I shall refer to him as Jorge J. in this book to differentiate him from Dad.

As a baby, my brother had light red hair that made him very noticeable among other children wherever we went. I can remember being intensely jealous when people would ooh and aah over him because he was so much more American-looking than I. His hair later turned as dark as mine, so it was no longer an issue when we were older.

The Great Depression was a worldwide calamity by the time Jorge J. was born. The Philippines suffered terribly during that era; the country was underdeveloped and poverty-stricken in the best of economic times and the thirties only deepened its privations. My father's company depended almost entirely on the United States to buy its sugar and when a U.S. trade quota restricted sugar imports from anywhere but Hawaii and the Caribbean, sugar mills in the Philippines had to shut down. The Montilla Sugar Company was one of the casualties.

Without work and company housing, my father moved us into a rented house in nearby Isabela. Fortunately, my mother's frugal nature had seen to it that they had enough savings to sustain us, at least for a while, while

Dad spent months looking for work. He even joined a group of would-be homesteaders who traveled to Mindanao, the big island south of Negros, where free land was being offered on much the same plan as the 1880s Oklahoma Land Rush. The land-seekers went by sailboat because none of them could afford a steamer ticket.

I believe there was an underlying political motive in the free land program. The government was concerned about the number of Japanese immigrants who had begun farming in Mindanao. Many of them were brought into the country by American fruit corporations from California and Hawaii cognizant of the Japanese work ethic and the suitability of the fertile Mindanaon soil for pineapple fields. For the Japanese nationals, who were starved for farming space in their own country, the untilled valleys in the southern Philippines were as enticing as gold mines. And it was no secret that Japan intended to take control of all of the Pacific world.

Furthermore, Mindanao's native population was historically Moslem and the Philippine government in Manila faced from time to time the issue of restoring the peace when Moro *datus,* angered by their Christian neighbors, stirred up their clans to engage in beheadings. Federal officials hoped that inducing more Catholic and Protestant Filipino families to settle in Mindanao, by offering them homesteads, would solve both the Japanese and the Moslem dilemmas.

The prospect of farming land of his own was quite an enticement for Jorge Madamba. His father's fields in northern Luzon were not vast enough to sustain the number of heirs who would inherit them, and Jorge's training in modern agriculture would be rejected by those who didn't like change. But after a week or two in Mindanao, checking out the political lay of the land and the cultural climate, Dad came home to Negros without staking a claim.

"I don't think the Moros would be friendly to us," my father told my mother. "Moslem women don't go out without their husbands, you know. Their clothing covers their whole bodies except their eyes. They don't wear men's trousers when they ride horseback. I think it would not be safe for you and the children to live there. Helen already reads books and Jorge Judy has white skin."

In 1939, Dad was called into the Philippine Constabulary, the national guard, to train a defense force against an imminent invasion by Japan. He was sent to an army post on the island of Samar and Mother was on her own to support herself and two small children in a land where she didn't know the language and had no other family members to share her tribulations. To say that Dad's military salary was meager is an understatement.

Encouraged by some American friends who lived in the capital city of Bacolod, Mom advertised her skill as a cake baker to make ends meet. She made wonderful cakes, including angel foods containing a dozen or more hand-whipped egg whites, which she baked in a wood-burning oven during days when the humidity was dense enough to make brownies fall. To this day, I swoon over the scent of vanilla and a beautiful airy angel food cake turned out on a crystal platter. Mother took commissions to make cakes for celebrations put on by local wealthy families. The cake itself was not important to the hosts; they would have been just as pleased with a plaster of Paris facsimile that would never bear cutting, much less eating, as long as it was ostentatiously and colorfully decorated.

Mother was not a cake decorator. She didn't know anything about making spun sugar resemble crystal clouds and wreaths of flowers and fountains spraying translucent pastel candy streamers into the air. On at least one occasion I recall, a cake was sent back to Mother for a rehab. She scraped off the seven-minute frosting and the powdered-sugar daisies that she'd piped onto the rim of the cake, and she tried to make it fancier but she probably never was paid for her inadequate attempts at high-style baking.

Having failed at cake catering, Mother did the thing that was most natural for her. She moved us out onto the land. She rented a small plot of ground near Libas, another rural village in the area. There we lived in a rustic but fairly comfortable two-room home built high on bamboo stilts. Iva Harrison was now getting a different glimpse of life in the real Philippines. For her, though, there was joy in being surrounded by a garden created by her own labor—sweet potatoes, peppers, tomatoes, spinach, squash, cucumbers, beans, peanuts, and corn. We had eggs and chickens and pork from our homegrown pigs. We picked wild guavas for jelly, and ripe mangoes and avocados from trees in our dooryard. For breakfast we ate papayas and great pink pomelos we called Chinese oranges. Bananas were plentiful—several varieties to be eaten out of hand, and cooking bananas, now called plantains. Mom made soap from rendered pork lard and lye derived from wood ash, and traded it, along with her surplus produce, for fish and shellfish from seaside peddlers. The skills she had were inherited from her mother and passed on by her five older sisters, her brother Marshall, and the farmers of northwest Oklahoma. She did, however, acquire a new culinary technique that my brother and I enjoy to this day. She learned to make *tapa*, which is carabao beef dried over a smoky fire, and salted dried fish. We now call those two delicacies jerky and anchovies.

Christmas of 1939, in the depths of the Depression, saw us making a Christmas tree out of a tropical shrub. First we stripped the shrub of all its broad green leaves, then we wrapped its branches in green crepe paper, which Mother had cut into fringes. Since neither Jorge J. nor I could remember seeing a real evergreen, the ersatz version was every bit as satisfactory as a Douglas fir. I am told there are pines in the mountains of Baguio but I was just two when my parents took me there on vacation and my brother had never been in northern Luzon. So we created one of our own and festooned it with strings of berries and bits of tinfoil and shards of glass that Mother had saved from jars and crockery accidentally broken during the year. Tin can lids also made lovely tree ornaments, and my brother and I added our original drawings and folded paper mobiles to the holiday trimmings.

Because we had so much fun making our beautiful tree, Mother let us decorate another one just like it. We carried it down the hill to a family with little children who lived in a hut even tinier than ours. Mother wrapped a box of cookies she'd made during the day to present with the tree. It was a Christmas Eve surprise for our neighbors and I shall never forget the sound of the children's laughing voices as we carried the tree into their house.

4

A Child before the War

/ / /

After six months in army camp on Samar, my father was released from active duty and he came home to Negros. Shortly afterward, he had the good fortune to land a job with another sugar corporation, Victorias Milling Company, based in the city of Manapla in northern Negros Occidental. The new position was not directly related to sugar production. Instead, Dad was hired to manage a rice plantation at the far southern end of the island, where in addition to its substantial number of hectares of rice, Victorias Milling also owned a thriving grove of coconut trees. The company exported copra—dried coconut—which would ultimately be made into cooking oil and livestock feed, and would form the base ingredient for various cosmetics and other products we didn't know anything about. Having grown up in the rice fields of Ilocos Norte, my father was delighted with his duties. His main interest as an agriculture student at Oklahoma A&M was the hybridization of new strains of grain, and in this instance, rice, for improved growth, higher yield, and better nutritional value.

The only drawback to Dad's new job was that the plantation was far beyond the borders of modern civilization. The only highway on Negros ended many miles from where we would live, and so did electricity, telephone lines, regular mail service, and schools, hospitals, and medical care. Our new home could be reached only by boat or walking trail. Otherwise, our timely contact with the outside world would be by short-wave radio—when it worked. For my mother and father, this situation was the best they could hope for, given the precarious state of affairs throughout the globe, but knowing my parents, I believe they saw it as another challenge.

Dad's new bosses were the Ossorio family, whose name indicated they were descendants of seventeenth-century grandees who owned enormous holdings on Negros Island and throughout the Philippines. In the early days of colonization by Spain, King Philip granted patents of land to his subjects who ventured into the New World to claim its riches for the Spanish Empire. Through five centuries, those who continued the Spanish lineage kept the land holdings intact within the families. I've been told the Ossorios were among the first families, although at least two of the young Ossorios in charge of the family operations in the mid-twentieth century were married to American women.

In Negros during the 1930s, labor was cheap, sugar cane was easy to grow, and rice, the staple food of the Filipino worker, could be sold in company stores to employees at lower than retail cost. Hence the planta-tion owned and operated by Victorias Milling in the hinterlands of the south was a profitable adjunct to sugar production.

We moved to Cartagena in early 1940. It was more than thirty miles past the end of the island's only vehicle-passable road. The small town of Cauayan was our last outpost for mechanized transportation and communi-cation. After Cauayan, travelers going south either hiked through the jungle and along the beach, or sailed by outrigger *banca*. The journey was a day or two long or more, depending on the weather and the energy level of the travelers. We were at the ends of the earth.

But my parents were not strangers to that romantic form of living. I think they might have been excited about a life in the wild, where they had no need to be concerned about conventional opinion, and where they could be in control of their own lifestyle, their own destiny. My mother, after all, was taken as an infant by her parents on a railroad train to Oklahoma Territory before statehood and she grew up in a house built of prairie sod. She was the first of her family—certainly the first woman—to finish college. The students she taught in her one-room schoolhouse who are still living, now in their late eighties and nineties, speak of her as a model of fearlessness. My father, too, followed a renegade path. He was a trailblazer for any number of young Asians who would decide to explore the Western world and return to change some of the feudal practices of their homelands.

Our first two years in Cartagena were the most serene epoch of all my life. They were like living a tale out of a book of South Sea stories. Victorias Milling provided us a lovely Greek Revival-style house of clapboard siding painted gray, with a second-story balcony and a veranda beneath overlooking the beach and the Sulu Sea. Our front lawn was surrounded by a hedge of ever-blooming hibiscus that provided us with color even more vivid than the sunsets we enjoyed almost every evening. My brother and I each had an upstairs bedroom and there was a real bathroom on the second floor, although the plumbing never worked very well. Our servants had to carry buckets of water up the stairs for the bathtub and the toilet tank. We used towels and washcloths freely—Mother no longer had to do the laundry—and we brushed our teeth and slept in four-poster beds with pillows and sheets and net canopies to protect us from malaria-carrying mosquitoes. Our dining table was set with linen and china and we had a cook, a laundress, gardeners, and a general housekeeper named Picar. The company paid their salaries.

Our little community, Cartagena, consisted of the company house that we occupied and a dozen or so nipa shacks along paths in the sand where the tenant families lived. Our front door was a few yards from the edge of the Sulu Sea, the main body of water through the islands of the Philippines that separated them from the open Pacific Ocean. While our mother watched us from the veranda, my brother and I spent hours each day in the surf with our friends, the children of the tenant farmers. We were on first-name terms with their families, who fished during the evening and early morning, bringing in catches of crab and *langosta*—small lobsters or large shrimp—tuna, squid, eel, and other more exotic varieties of seafood whose names I no longer recall. When the waves were calm and the weather was balmy, and especially when the moon was full and the night glowed with silver light, we would go out with our friends in their family bancas and look down at the coral-colored world many meters beneath the surface of the sea where magnificent marine animals entertained us with their silent hypnotic ballet.

Other times during the day, Jorge J. and I scampered across the ties of the narrow-gauge railroad bridge that spanned the lagoon separating our house on the beach from the mainland. We played among the nipa palms of the swamp around the lagoon and clambered over rusted remains of what had once been gold or copper mining machinery that had been abandoned in a failed venture years before.

Occasionally, we would go to the fields with our dad, trailing after him as he inspected the rice crops and spoke with the tenant farmers, advising them on the proper levels of irrigation and the ratio of seedling rice that they should use on each paddy. We particularly enjoyed our forays with our father when we could ride on the railroad handcart that was used to bring in gunnysacks of rice at harvest.

I learned to read when I was five, so I spent much of my time with the books Mother and Dad brought home to me. In 1941 I was eight years old and by American standards I should have been in the third grade. Because the nearest public school was an hour's hike from our house, my parents were reluctant to send me off to a strange community to study in a classroom with children and a teacher they did not know. The best private boarding school in the Philippines was in Baguio, days of travel away in Luzon. Its tuition was extremely high, and neither of my parents was willing to put us in the care of an unknown authority within the, to them, unfamiliar Episcopal Church. It's a bittersweet thought that I now am an Episcopalian and have been for forty years, a conversion decision that I made as an adult while I was living in Northern California.

In August of 1941, my parents reconsidered and enrolled me in the public school nearest Cartagena. I don't remember much about it except that on the way home after school each day, I longed to spend a centavo or two for a snack at the Chinese *sari-sari* (a precursor of today's convenience store deli) because my schoolmates did. What really enticed me was a pastry that resembled what I know now as a crepe with some sort of cream filling. My dad warned me sternly not to eat anything that was sold on the street, no matter how hungry I was or how delicious it looked. His concern about my gastrointestinal health was understandable, even if I didn't appreciate it at the time. I took his word for it and never went against his edict.

My school career was short-lived when Pearl Harbor was bombed and World War II began in December. The public schools lacked government funding and were closed to allow parents to keep their children at home for safety's sake. We had no idea when the Japanese would invade our island, but invasion seemed inevitable.

Mother, however, didn't miss a beat. We had books and pencils and paper at home and she proceeded to organize my brother and me into a structured classroom. We even had a few classmates who came in to take advantage of my mother's tutoring, but that didn't last long because our schedules were sporadic at best.

Perhaps we didn't have a full six-period day of study but all told, Jorge J. and I were in a learning mode throughout our waking hours. Mother read to us, we read to each other, I read to myself. We learned to look at the flora and fauna of the island, the weather changes on the ocean and among the palm trees, the shapes and colors of the seashells we gathered on our Sulu beach, the stars that clustered around the Southern Cross in the gathering nighttime. Mother taught us to sing. Although we had no instruments to accompany ourselves, we could harmonize with our voices. Sometimes one or another neighbor or house servant would come out on the veranda with his mandolin or guitar and that music transported us beyond the horizon of our dreams. My father loved music and loved to dance.

5

Our Dear Friend Picar

/ / /

In Cartagena we had a succession of nursemaids, housemaids, kitchen helpers, seamstresses, laundresses, and general maintenance workers, both men and women. I liked most of them but none as much as Picar. I loved Picar.

If my mother had one true, best Filipina friend, it was Picar. Picar was animated, bright and witty. She learned English with ease, spoke it well, and actually discussed ideas in it with Mom. Picar worked just as diligently as my mother. She was up at dawn to light the fire in the kitchen stove so it would be ready for Mother to cook breakfast. She checked the laundry, lined out the housecleaning, made sure everything was in its place. She kept the household running like a finely wound clock. Best of all, she was the closest to a traditional amah, a nurse-governess, that I would ever have. Before long, Picar was our full-fledged house manager.

She was a godsend for my mother. After she had been with us for a while, Picar took on many responsibilities that Mother would never have allowed anyone else to assume. Our parents trusted her so much, they even went away on trips together, to the north of Negros, leaving Jorge J. and me in Picar's care at home in Cartagena.

Picar saw to it that we behaved while Dad and Mom were away. She cooked our favorite meals and kept us neat and clean. She told us stories in both Visayan and English and sang to us and made us go to bed when it was time. Picar was the only servant we ever had who kept us in line, who taught us self-discipline and corrected us when we misbehaved.

One of the few things about my mother that troubled her Filipina employees was her American version of child discipline. Filipino parents didn't spank their children for punishment or let them cry in pain or humiliation. The poorest, most underprivileged child was cuddled and carried about if he or she was unhappy. Our childhood friends did not fight amongst themselves or talk back to their parents or throw temper tantrums on the floor. Even adolescents at that time were respectful, soft-spoken and happy-faced in the presence of their elders and peers alike.

Although Mother would never dream of hurting us, she did expect us to be accountable and she wasn't hesitant about spanking when she thought it necessary. There were times when Jorge J. and I exasperated her to the point that she found a switch and made it sting our legs for a moment or so. I don't suppose it ever occurred to Mom that the Filipino way of raising children could be better than hers. She was concerned that my brother and I would be overindulged and lazy, unable to fend for ourselves and dependent on subordinates to see to our comfort and cater to our convenience. Mother had reason for her feelings. In some of the upscale families that we knew, the children were helpless and demanding. In her certainty that we would one day live in the United States, our mother was making sure that we would be self-reliant, independent, and able to take care of ourselves on our own.

Our servants were sternly instructed not to wait on Jorge J. and me. Had they not been so directed, our slightest whimper would have been catered to and our demands instantly gratified. New employees were cautioned by their experienced predecessors that in our peculiar American household we children could howl and fight and argue with each other, but if either of us showed disrespect or meanness to our caregivers, we were quickly reprimanded. I know our household help appreciated Mother's sensitivity for their feelings. However, on the rare occasion when our mother smacked our bottoms and let us wail, the nursemaids muttered among themselves and shook their heads in disapproval.

My mother set the disciplinary rules and saw to it that they were carried out, but my father was a cream puff. Only once was he ever really so angry with me that he would have inflicted punishment. It happened while we were still living in Tinongan and I was about three, which shows that such a rare occurrence really made an impression on me. One afternoon Dad was holding my infant brother in a big wicker rocking chair, lulling him off to sleep. Wanting to be part of the action, I plunked myself down heavily on one of the chair rockers, tipping both my dad and my tiny brother over onto the floor. Neither of them was hurt in the spill, fortunately, and I jumped away in time to avoid being hit by the rocking chair but Dad was livid. He grabbed a hairbrush and chased me through the house, roaring with anger. I don't remember his catching up with me and I doubt that he would have applied the hairbrush if he had. Most likely he turned me over to Mother, who would have punished with the flat of her hand on my rear.

Jorge J. and I learned early that our father would give us anything we asked for. Dad was an incorrigible gift-giver by nature and with us he knew no restraints. Only Mother's powerful right of veto saved him from gifting us into the poorhouse. It was Dad who brought us pretty things he found when he was on trips away from home. He bought us toys and candy, silk fans and picture books for me, and baseball bats and balls and great bronze swords for my brother. Mother's gifts were clothes that would not shrink or fade, that would wear forever and were always too big, because we would "grow into them," she said. Mother's measure of the value of any purchase was whether or not it was "practical"—long after I was an adult, she justified whatever she gave me by terming it "practical." Only in the last year or two have I used that word, and I cringe when I buy a bunch of cut flowers at the supermarket and tell myself they are "practical."

Picar, our housekeeper, followed Mother's lead and was firm and had no compunctions about scolding us when it was necessary. Picar had completed the seventh grade, which at that time in the Philippines was the final year of grammar school, and I doubt that she'd had any further schooling. But she was an inveterate reader. She read our English-language books and magazines and the *Manila Daily Bulletin*, which came in, seven editions at a time, by mail boat once a week. Picar also had subscriptions to Visayan publications, which she took to her room to read during her siesta.

I was intensely curious about Picar's reading matter. Occasionally, she would allow me into her room to look at magazine pictures of high fashion clothes and movie stars. One day I happened by her open door and saw a tabloid newspaper lying on her bed. Picar was elsewhere in the house but I went into her room, knowing full well it was not allowed. Mother had laid down a very strict rule forbidding us from invading our servants' private quarters. I picked up the Visayan-language periodical that must have been a Filipino version of *National Enquirer* or *True Confessions*, and read it front to back, fascinated, for half an hour.

Picar came upon me as I was reading and she gave me a tongue-lashing even my mother could not have matched. She was furious because I had gone into her room uninvited, her sanctum, the only place in the world she could call her own, and she was mortified that I'd read the newspaper, which was hardly fit for a seven-year-old's eyes. More than anything, Picar was angry with me because she feared my curiosity might cost her job.

There was some justification in her fear. Had my mother known I had access to such lurid literature, she would have been very upset. Although Mother would not have had a clue what I'd read, there were pictures in the publication that all too graphically illustrated what the stories were about. Picar made sure after that to keep her X-rated reading material out of sight and, sadly, I was deprived of the opportunity to become more literate the printed Visayan language.

A year or so later, I came across a paperback version of *For Whom the Bell Tolls* that my mother had carelessly left on her bedside table. She was devastated because I was transfixed with Hemingway's story and she was particularly concerned about my reading the episode in which Robert and Maria share a sleeping bag. I didn't understand why she objected so much to that part of the story.

Picar fell in love with Esteban, my father's warehouse foreman—and it was a good thing because even I detected that Dad was drawn to Picar's vivacity, her industrious nature, and her sunny disposition. Mother was glad that Picar had found her true love and Esteban was a very good match for her. He was a hardworking, stable, and serious young man in whom my father placed great trust. In the old tradition, Esteban went to my father, the Mister, and asked his permission for Picar's hand in marriage, which was granted.

Our friend the Roman Catholic priest Father Oomun officiated at the nuptials in Picar's family home in the next village. Because Picar's father was deceased, my dad gave the bride away. Esteban moved into Picar's room in the servants' quarters and my parents felt even more secure about leaving us when they traveled to company headquarters up north. The Ossorio brothers and cousins met with my father three or four times a year to hear his report on the rice plantation's operation, and it was an opportunity for Mother to stock up on staples such as canned milk, flour and sugar, household goods, sewing fabric, and the next size in shoes for Jorge J. and me.

A few months after Picar and Esteban were married, something started to go wrong. I sensed that my parents were whispering behind closed doors and I overheard some of their conversation. Then one day, they told us that Picar and Esteban were leaving. I could not understand why Mom and Dad were letting them go.

"It's Esteban's health," my mother said. She was trying to be gentle in telling us. "He is coughing a lot, coughing up blood, and I'm afraid he has tuberculosis."

I was heartbroken. If Esteban were ill and had to leave, why did Picar have to leave too, I asked. "She can stay, can't she, Mom?" I pleaded. "Please, please, don't let Picar go away."

"No," said my mother. "Her place is with Esteban. He needs her now and where he goes, she must also go."

They left the next day. They stood in our front doorway to tell us good-bye, a couple of pitiful suitcases in their hands. Picar embraced us, weeping. I wanted to run after them and ask them to take me with them. Mother and Dad would not let me follow them out the door.

Sometime after that, I saw Picar and Esteban one more time. I walked into my father's office one day and they were there. Esteban was no longer the muscular young man who married Picar. His face was pasty gray and his once-strong shoulders were stooped and withered. His jaunty, agile frame had become gaunt; he was a scarecrow of a man, terribly ill.

Picar was speaking to my father, pleadingly. She stopped when she saw me come in.

"Picar," I screamed, rushing to throw myself into her arms. "Picar, you've come back!"

She drew away from me. "No," she said. "No. Don't come close to me."

"Go outside, Helen," said my father. "Picar and Esteban are just leaving. They can't visit with you. Go outside and don't bother us."

Except in the most serious situations, my father always called me "Jiggs." I knew better than to argue with him now.

I crept out of my father's office and watched them walk away, Esteban leaning on Picar for support as he shuffled along. She never looked back at me. She took her husband's arm and led him past the hibiscus hedge that bordered our yard, and they trudged out onto the road to the valley.

I never saw her again.

6

Father Oomun

/ / /

Father Oomun was a big man, at least six feet tall, with great muscles, rosy-faced, yellow-haired, and deep-voiced. He exuded warmth and love of life and gentle compassion with brilliant sparkle in his Dutch-blue eyes. He always dressed in a starched white cassock. My brother and I wondered if he had trousers on under his ankle-length robe. We peered surreptitiously at his laundry but we never did determine what he wore beneath his vestment.

Father Oomun, our friend in 1940 and 1941, was a Roman Catholic circuit-riding priest. I don't know what order he belonged to but it didn't matter to us. We were Protestants. Although mother was skeptical about Catholicism in general, she was charmed by Father Oomun when he sat down at her table, spending a full hour or so savoring her fried chicken and gravy and biscuits, her yams cooked in brown sugar and coconut milk, and her homemade noodles, sweet corn on the cob, sliced cucumber salad with home-grown tomatoes, and crisp new radishes, green onions, and lima beans. When she brought out a devil's food cake at the end of the meal and Father Oomun ate half of it with a beatific smile on his face, she was as worshipful as any of his most devout parishioners.

My parents looked forward to Father Oomun's visits from his parish headquarters church in Cauayan because he brought news of the world. He knew much more about what was going on than we could read in the *Manila Daily Bulletin*. Father Oomun had the inside word on what was happening with Hitler and Stalin, Mussolini, Premier Tojo, and whether or not the Poles were going to make it through the winter. He was our best source of information about world affairs because he was a ham radioman, and he presented the day's events to us with greater flair than any newscaster. I listened to him with rapt attention every time he came to our house on his periodic rounds of his vast mission region. Of course, my parents offered him a place to stay, an offer he could not refuse although we were not members of his congregation. After all, how could anyone turn down my mother's cinnamon rolls for breakfast?

"Ve vil hel-up the Rossians," he would announce, stepping out of his outboard-motorized banca. "Ve vill anhihilate dose Chermans. You vait, dey von't last through Easter, dose svine."

Father Oomun was from Amsterdam and his animosity toward Nazi Germany knew no bounds.

"Roosewelt is a covard," he proclaimed. "Poor Vinston Churchill, vat can he do? Dunkirk—his men are lost, no supplies, no guns, no boats, nutting vith vitch to fight. Roosewelt vas born of my countryvolk but he vas not a friend to the poor English, the poor Dutch."

Father Oomun did not subscribe to the belief that the clergy should stand aside in political matters. He spoke his mind without fear of offending those who might not agree with him.

He came to our part of the island every two or three months to conduct Mass, baptize babies, confirm the converts, serve First Communion to the youngsters, and say the Requiem for the dead. Most importantly, he performed the sacrament of marriage for dozens of couples who had been waiting for him to come and bless their unions.

I was allowed to attend his services on one of the days of his multiple weddings. There were ten or twelve sets of brides and grooms joining in matrimony in one simultaneous exchange of vows. I will never forget the spectacle of it all. Some of the brides were dressed in traditionally Western white lace and silk and their bridegrooms wore dapper tuxedoes or formal Filipino barong tagalogs, the beautiful embroidered long-sleeved outshirts of sheer piña (cloth woven of pineapple fiber.) Other brides chose more flamboyant wedding ensembles reminiscent of showgirls, featuring red spangles and purple velvet in variations of design based on the Filipina mestiza and traditional Spanish Colonial Maria Clara dresses. Their families most likely had to sell a prize carabao to afford the finery. Several of the brides were obviously pregnant.

Father Oomun blessed them all in splendid solemnity, as if the vows were being said in a cathedral. His love and care for all the people who came to his church were evident, no matter that the church was a nipa-roofed shed with plank benches for pews, and the music consisted of a mandolin and a guitar.

We loved Father Oomun because he played with us as if he were a child himself. He spent afternoons on the beach with us, racing up and down the sand, swinging us up in the air in his bearlike arms as his white cotton cassock flapped in the seawater. We played tag, made sand castles, and he taught us to draw Dutch words with sticks at the water's edge.

His voice boomed, "I vill count vun, two, tree. I vill cower my eyes but I know vere you are. Behind da coconut tree—I vill find you."

My brother and I and our friends giggled and squealed and did our best to outwit him but Father Oomun was never outdone. He had as much energy as we did, and as the afternoon wore on and our mother called us up to the house to wash up for dinner, he would sling the two of us over his shoulders and gallop up the beach slope, joyfully singing a rousing Dutch drinking song.

Jorge J. and I had the benefit of having the world's biggest swimming hole in our front yard. Unless it was raining, we spent our time in or near the Pacific Ocean. Sometimes storms would come through and leave waves that pounded the shoreline in huge swells and troughs that weren't safe to swim in, but we had no fear of the water. On one occasion, I was playing at the edge of the sand, letting the incoming waves chase me up the beach. Because I was showing off for Father Oomun, who was watching us, I stayed a moment too long and a high wave swamped me and carried me back into the surf. Trying to stay afloat, I bobbed up and down, realizing I couldn't touch bottom, gulping mouthfuls of seawater in my panic.

Father Oomun's voice came out to me over the roar of the waves as he waded out quickly to grab me before the next swell rose over us both. "Don't be afraid," he shouted. "Keep calm. I vill hel-up you. I'm coming. I vill hel-up you."

He plucked me out of the sea and carried me head down onto the beach. What seemed like a gallon of seawater drained out of my throat.

I never knew anything about Father Oomun's family in Holland or how his ministry had brought him to the far Pacific. His zest for life and his curiosity about the countryside, his genuine joy in the people he served, and his concern about the suffering that would surely result from war left a lasting impression on my eight-year-old mind.

After dinner, my brother and I went upstairs to bed, and I went to sleep listening to Father Oomun's great voice from the dining room, discussing the state of the world with my parents. They talked about critical issues of the time, including Roosevelt's New Deal and how it was rescuing America from the Depression. In this instance, Father Oomun agreed with the president and spoke with pride of Roosevelt's Dutch ancestry. He told my parents of the desperate need of the Jews in Europe for our "hel-up," which he learned from his ham radio friends.

Most of all, my mother and father listened carefully to Father Oomun's assessment of the possibility of war with Japan. Although they probably never expressed it, I think they wanted to ask Father Oomun, "What will happen to us when we are invaded? How will we be treated, how can we protect our two little children? Who will help us?"

Father Oomun told us about his ham radio set-up in the rectory of his church. It was his pride and joy and he seemed to be updating it constantly with the latest technology. "I talked to Vladivostok last night," he told us. Then he'd say, "My friend in Mississippi said to me da riwer hass broken t'rough da lewee again," or "Do you know how cold it vas in Nome, Alaska, last veek? Forty-sewen degrees below zero, Farenheit! Shust tink about dat."

To reciprocate my parents' hospitality, Father Oomun fixed things mechanical that were out of order. He adjusted the damper on Mother's wood-burning range, he worked on the gears of the hand-car that brought the bags of harvested rice to the beach on our two-mile hand-powered narrow-gauge railway. He repaired the compressor on our Servel refrigerator, and said to my brother and me, "Now vatch. Tonight—vait and see—ve vill haf ice cream. Vat do you vant—chocolate or wanilla or banana?"

He was always sending off for things in the mail—radio parts, engine mountings for the outboard motor of his boat, modifications for our windcharger. He brought with him when he came a modest stash of Scotch whiskey, sherry for my mother, and Dutch beer for Dad. Sometimes my father joined him in a small glass of Scotch, liberally laced with well water, while Mom nervously sipped a thimbleful of sherry.

After spending two or three days with us, Father Oomun continued his trip south to see another group of his widespread congregation and extend his pastoral service to them. Reluctantly, we saw him off. He climbed into his motorized banca, pulled the engine cord, and putt-putted out to sea.

After Pearl Harbor, we never saw Father Oomun again. He simply disappeared. My father tried to locate him, stopping to inquire about him whenever he passed through Cauayan during the war. None of his parishioners knew where he was, or if they did they would not divulge his whereabouts, even to a trusted guerrilla leader. Until the Japanese sent occupation troops to Negros, Father Oomun continued his pastoral duties; it was surmised he might have been recalled to Manila by his church superiors. We also heard through the bamboo telegraph, or grapevine, that Father Oomun concealed his ham radio equipment in a cellar under the altar of the church. We were told the Japanese discovered the forbidden communication system and either shot the priest on the spot or took him into prison.

I've been haunted through the years by the thought that Father Oomun had made radio contact with the outside, perhaps Australia, perhaps even the United States. When Major Jess Villamor and his commandos landed on our beach, was it just coincidence that it was in my father's territory with my father's small band of guerrillas there to assist them? Father Oomun knew the tides, the sea depth, even the channels between the coral reefs in our Cartagena bay. When the submarine emerged to offload MacArthur's scouts, it had to be in a place where a rubber raft containing several men could safely get ashore, on a moonless night, without any sort of signal or landmark to guide them in.

I have given up ever knowing, but for the rest of my life I will remember Father Oomun's bright blue eyes, his unrestrained laughter, his big shoulders and magnificent height, and his booming voice calling across the waves, "Be calm. Don't be afraid. I vill hel-up you."

7

Aunt Charlotte

/ / /

Aunt Charlotte was a southern lady. She was not really my aunt but was my mother's best friend, so Jorge J. and I followed the Filipino custom of calling our parents' good friends "Aunt" or "Uncle" and even their children, "Cousin." In the Philippines, adults addressed their nearest and dearest friends as "compadre" and "comadre," which literally meant co-father and co-mother. It was wonderful evidence of the strong sense of community and family ties in the Filipino culture. Adults closely associated with a child took personal responsibility for co-parenting that child.

Aunt Charlotte and her husband, Uncle Segundo, lived in a beautiful house about twenty or twenty-five kilometers west of Isabela. Segundo was a chemical engineer and manager in charge of a sugar refinery in the town of Binalbagan. He and Charlotte married when he was studying sugar production at Louisiana State University.

A native of New Orleans, Aunt Charlotte spoke French and Spanish to her peers, and Visayan to her servants. When we visited Aunt Charlotte, we were served tea by maids dressed in pale blue uniforms with lace-trimmed white organdy aprons. Being in Aunt Charlotte's home was an awesome experience.

At our house, our egalitarian western Oklahoma mother taught my brother and me to set our own table and fetch our own snacks and bring our own dishes to the sink when we finished eating. Our household help wore their own regular clothes to work. They assisted with the heavy chores but Jorge J. and I made our beds, bathed and dressed ourselves, combed our own hair, and brushed our own teeth. We kept our play areas neat and clean—or as much so as possible for a six-year-old and a three-year-old.

At Aunt Charlotte's, the whole world was different. She ran her ménage like an antebellum southern mansion, and when I was there, before the war, Aunt Charlotte's maids tucked me into bed at night, laid out my clothes for the next morning, poured my orange juice and brought my choice of breakfast, picked up my toys, took me to the park and played my childish games with me the whole time we were there, served me lunch and dinner on a tray in the solarium (a word I could not spell until I was an adult), bathed me at night, flushed the toilet in my private bathroom after it was used, and sat with me to turn out the light after I had gone to sleep.

It was heavenly, being at Aunt Charlotte's. In her house there were embroidered Egyptian cotton sheets, crystal goblets on tall stems, fresh flowers on every table, and a special room called the library, lined on all four walls with books on shelves. The lower shelves were filled with children's books and there was even a window seat strewn with fluffy pillows where I could sit and read for as long as I liked. For me, it was heaven, all right.

The rooms in the living area of Aunt Charlotte's home all had ceiling fans and silken sofa throws and candelabra. (They had electricity, provided by the refinery generator.) Charlotte and Segundo owned a Victrola and they took the *Saturday Evening Post*, *Ladies Home Journal*, and *Harper's Magazine*. It was a culinary adventure, being at Aunt Charlotte's. That's where I first ate olives. Even my mother had never before tasted olives; she had only seen them in jars in Boehm's Grocery in Woodward, Oklahoma, where she worked before she came to the Philippines. Aunt Charlotte served warm Swiss cheese on Melba toast, oolong tea in translucent porcelain cups, chilled vichyssoise, roasted chestnuts, tiny cornichon, French wine and profiteroles, bonbons and chocolate mousse, and asparagus.

Aunt Charlotte had pale green eyes and naturally graying ash-blonde hair, decades before postmenopausal women in America colored their aging hair ash-blonde. She was the grandest of grande dames with a wonderful sense of humor, unassailable in the faces of the really wealthy Filipino matrons who intimidated my mother. Charlotte wore white linen dresses, white silk stockings, and high-heeled opera pumps even in the vilest of humid weather. She was short—about five feet two—and inclined to plumpness. Her whole appearance was in sharp contrast to that of my raw-boned, tall, freckled, almost-red-haired mother, who dressed mostly in khaki culottes, ordinary cotton shirts, and flat, sensible, size 10 shoes.

How Aunt Charlotte and my mother ever found anything in common, I never will understand. My mother detested social one-upmanship. She scorned idleness and sloth and extravagance and anything ostentatious. Mother was uncomfortable at fancy parties, uneasy in opulent settings, fidgety in social rituals and completely out of touch with society gossip. My mother felt guilty if anyone, much less a servant, did "her work" and she was never patient enough to let anyone do anything she knew she could do herself.

My aunt Charlotte was none of those things. She lived in what seemed to me splendor, commanding the social schedule of the province. She was on a first-name basis with the governor and his wife, and his mother and his mother-in-law. She visited regularly with the archbishop (as a Louisianan, of course, she was Roman Catholic.) She knew the highest-ranking military leader in the province, the patriarchs and matriarchs of the oldest families, the most moneyed stratum of power on that Croesus-rich island. Aunt Charlotte was an active participant in its political feuds, its society games, its business deals (and double deals), its interminable family squabbles that spanned decades and generations. She played mah jong and bridge with women whose last names were Vargas, Roxas, del Pilar, Aquino, and Sotomayor. Aunt Charlotte called José Laurel, "Joe." She became friendly with him on her frequent trips to Manila, where two of her three children were in convent boarding school. Laurel was later installed as the puppet president of the Philippines by the Japanese occupation.

I can only speculate that Aunt Charlotte and my mother recognized in each other a commonality in their motives, their ambition, their solid American backgrounds, and their uncompromising approach to living. Aunt Charlotte gave no quarter and neither did my mother. Aunt Charlotte always referred to her native city as "N'Yawlins." Mother pronounced it "New-erleens." However, I never ever heard Aunt Charlotte call my mother an Okie. The term probably had not yet achieved worldwide usage.

I doubt that Aunt Charlotte and her family were all that more affluent than we were. They just knew how to live well. Occasionally, I would hear my mother comment to my father about Aunt Charlotte's uppityness, especially with her servants, and her snobby views on everything. No one could ever tell Aunt Charlotte anything she didn't already know about the state of the world, about religion, about the raising of children or the management of a household. She had the final word on everything. I think Mother must have alternately feared and envied Aunt Charlotte for her urban southern sophistication and earthy interest in everything that was going on, but at the same time she recognized the essential goodness of her best friend.

We saw Aunt Charlotte once after Pearl Harbor when Jorge J., Mother, and I traveled north to spend a few days with Dad at his military base. Charlotte's daughters were still in Manila, three hundred miles away by sea, and Manila was under siege. Understandably, Charlotte was terribly worried. Her friends in high places assured her the girls were safe in Manila because it was heavily fortified and because there was a large American colony living there. And surely the convent school, with its contingent of fearless nuns, was as secure as any place could be in the Philippines.

Three times a day, Aunt Charlotte put on a veil and went to church to say novenas for the safety of her children. It was touching, heart-rending, and disturbing to see our self-confident "aunt" brought to her knees, pleading for God's intervention.

When the Japanese came to Negros, we learned that Aunt Charlotte was ordered to Bacolod to be interned in the concentration camp there. But she charmed the Japanese camp commander, and using her influence with the rich and powerful Filipinos who were in the occupation government, she was allowed to rent a home outside the camp, where she was confined to house arrest. My father remarked, "I hope Charlotte doesn't get herself into trouble. She'd better keep her mouth shut and try not to lord it over the Japanese."

We knew nothing else about Aunt Charlotte's fate until my father heard something on the bamboo telegraph in 1944. He told my mother about it late in the night when he thought I was asleep.

"Charlotte was caught spying," he said in a shaking voice. "She was hanged by the Japanese."

8

Pearl Harbor

/ / /

The Madamba family celebrated Christmas of 1941 on or about December 12, not December 25.

Pearl Harbor in Hawaii and Clark Field in the Philippines were bombed to smithereens on December 8 and 9 on the western side of the International Dateline. We did not know about the attack until days afterward, and when we did learn that the United States and the Philippines were at war with Japan, my parents hastily planned a Christmas celebration for the next day. My father was a second lieutenant in the United States Army Reserve as well as a member of the Philippine defense force, which already had been rolled into the U.S. Armed Forces in the Far East (USAFFE). Dad packed his gear and made arrangements to join his unit at Headquarters in northern Negros the day after.

Jorge J. and I crept down the stairs on our "Christmas morning" and gazed in wonder at our Christmas tree and the gifts beneath it. Truly, Santa Claus had come during the night and left us the presents we had written for. My brother received a complete Tom Mix cowboy costume—chaps, Levis, western shirt trimmed with rivets and fringe, and a ten-gallon hat that fit perfectly. He was ecstatic with the additional gift of a pair of cap pistols, holsters, and several rolls of caps. (They didn't last long.) I was just as happy with a Betsy Wetsy doll with eyes that opened and closed, who cried and wet her diaper when she was fed. It may have been a premature Christmas but nonetheless we reveled in it.

Ironically, that was the year I surmised that Santa Claus was just another figure of mythology. My brother and I sneaked out of our beds to sit on the top step of the staircase and we peered through the banister to watch our parents arranging the gift-wrapped boxes. Even in my eight-year-old mind, I was touched to see the happiness in their faces as they placed our gifts so lovingly beneath the Christmas tree. It would be the last Christmas we would celebrate in a real house until 1945.

A few days earlier, I overheard some of the servants saying among themselves that there really wasn't a white-bearded man in a red suit coming in the middle of the night to distribute presents to us all, including them. At first it made me angry to think my parents would deceive me, and sad that there was no Santa Claus. But when I opened my presents I was too delighted with a new doll to be angry, so I played along with my parents' charade to make them happy too.

The cowboy suit and the doll came in a big box by mail from Sears Roebuck and Company in Chicago. I think Mother had ordered them out of the catalog the previous July. My mother's sister in Oklahoma, Aunt Mattie, sent us a box of clothes she had made for us, several dresses for me and some pants and shirts for Jorge J. Her gifts were a godsend. We were still wearing those same clothes, patched over and over again, with the last smidge of hem and seam let out, in 1945.

Dad left to fight the war the next day, wearing his uniform with his U.S. Army second lieutenant's bars shining and his boots polished to the luster of patent leather. He looked so dashing. He climbed into the motorized banca that would take him up north and we did not know whether or not he would be deployed to the fighting in Luzon. In her journal, my mother wrote that when he arrived at Negros headquarters, Dad had orders to report to Mindanao, where General MacArthur had assigned military units to make a last stand in the defense of the Philippines. Dad was sent on a one-day reconnaissance mission the day before his unit left for the south. He was still in the hills of Negros when his outfit left, so he was re-ordered to remain at the base in LaCarlota. Mother undoubtedly said a prayer of thanksgiving for that providential change of plan.

During those last weeks of December and through the early weeks of 1942, we had little idea of the destruction of the U.S. Navy fleet in Hawaii or even of the warfare going on in and around Manila. Whatever news we had, passed on by someone who had a short-wave radio, was probably carefully censored to prevent panic, and to avoid letting the enemy know how much the Japanese army had hurt us. I think my parents were as naïve as I was, thinking America would be able to shut down the Nippon military offensive within a month or two. We could not imagine that the United States was so committed to the European war that it would not send men and materiel to the Pacific.

"Any day now," we believed, "any day now the fight will be over on Luzon. MacArthur has thousands and thousands of troops and Corregidor [the island fortress that guarded Manila Harbor] is invincible."

Our first experience with combat occurred in January 1942 when Japanese bombers sank a U.S. Navy munitions ship that was hiding out during daylight hours in Miraculum Bay, just around the cove from Cartagena.

My brother and I were building sand forts along the lagoon behind our house that morning.

"Hear those airplanes coming in?" said my six-year-old brother. "I think they're Japs. They sound like washing machine motors."

Jorge J. must have gotten that phrase from Father Oomun. My brother had never seen or heard a washing machine motor. We continued with our fort construction for another few minutes, then the washing machine airplanes seemed to come in right over our heads. We saw the propellers whirring and felt the vibration of their engines on the sand beneath us. The red circles on their wings left no doubt what country they represented. Two or three of our friends were playing beside us, and simultaneously we dived under the cover of the broad nipa palms that bordered the lagoon. We crouched beneath the low-lying palms, holding our breath as we waited for the spatter of gunfire from the airplanes, but if they saw us, the pilots weren't interested at that moment in shooting children at play. The planes buzzed low over our beach, then flew over the ridge into Mira-calum and we heard the booms of exploding bombs.

It seemed as if the explosions continued for a long time, but it probably took only a few minutes to sink the ammunition freighter SS *Panay* to the bottom of the deep bay. Mother came to get us out of the nipa swamp and we were trembling with excitement over the closeness of the air attack. Although she didn't have much to say, I'm sure she praised us for our presence of mind in dashing under cover. Now that I've had my own exper-ience at motherhood, I imagine her knees and her voice were shaking.

The sinking of the *Panay* meant the loss of supplies and ammunition for the beleaguered U.S. and Philipine forces in Luzon. But no further military action occurred in the Visayas, so we were lulled into complacency for a few months. Three times, Mother and Jorge J. and I traveled north to the installation where my father was camp commander. We spent a few days each time enjoying the scenery and our father's attention. For me, the highlight of our trips was the mansion in which my father was billeted. The house was an estate of a very wealthy Chinese family who had moved away into one of their other homes and allowed the Philippine Army to use the beautiful residence. It was the grandest home I have ever seen. The grounds were formally landscaped, and even with a war on, meticulously groomed. The main house was immense. To call it imposing is an understatement.

Although the family's personal effects had been removed, the interior of the mansion was still palatial. There were tremendous carved rosewood doors, armoires, dressers, chests, tables, and armchairs fit for emperors and empresses. On the glistening mahogany floors were gorgeous rugs woven in glowing red and gold and deep green and pale blue silk and various wools. The balustrades were hand-carved teak, the chandeliers were tall tiers of crystal-like waterfalls, and the floor-to-ceiling windows were hung with damask silk. One could not enter a doorway into those rooms without a gasp of awe.

I thought to myself, "I could be comfortable, living here."

General Jonathan Wainwright, in great sorrow, surrendered the Philippines to the Japanese on May 6, 1942. His troops suffered and many died in the sixty-mile march from Bata-an to Cabanatuan prison near San Fernando, and in the conflagration of Corregidor. In Manila the concentration camps filled up—taking over Bilibid Federal Reformatory and Santo Tomas University, once one of the most prestigious liberal arts institutions of higher learning in the Far East. Most of the soldiers taken prisoners of war were young and Filipino; the rest were young and American. In the concentration camps were civilians—doctors, professors, industrialists, writers and journalists, priests and other ministers of faith, soldiers of fortune, and scientists, and their children. They were Americans, British, Dutch, Australians, New Zealanders, French, Scandinavians, and Canadians.

But Wainwright's soldiers and sailors didn't give up without a fight. The battles of Bata-an and Corregidor have been called the Alamo of World War II. In the Texas Alamo, Davy Crockett and Colonel Travis and Jim Bowie and a few dozen other Americans and Mexican-Americans and Native Americans held out against the Santa Ana army until the last man and woman died, while Sam Houston dithered about political strategy. At Bata-an and Corregidor, soldiers perished while American leadership was pre-occupied with the war in Europe. For all his power and personal magneticism, Douglas MacArthur had a hard time getting the United States' attention.

When the Philippines surrendered, my father was one of the last officers in his unit to leave the northern Negros cadre. With many of his men, Dad took to the hills after they destroyed all the camp's supplies and equipment to keep them from falling into the hands of the enemy. When civil and military leaders of Negros Occidental gave up the capital city, Bacolod, my father made his way south to arrange for us to go into hiding. I don't think my parents ever discussed the possibility of turning themselves in, at least not where I could hear them.

From January until the early summer of 1942, we continued to live on the beach because there seemed to be no effort on the Japanese Army's part to put troops on Negros. Because Dad was still on military duty, Mother took charge of the Cartagena rice plantation as well as a small rice farm of our own that my parents leased in the nearby community of Sipalay. (My father still clung to the dream that one day we would own our own land.)

In a letter written to her family in Ellis County, Oklahoma, dated November 15, 1942, and never sent, my mother said, "Our tenants are convinced that so long as the enemy did not station forces in our imme-diate vicinity, they should be working to produce food, so our rice fields are all planted." Iva Harrison was forever the farmer's daughter.

She added, "In the occupied portions of the province, little farm work [is being done]."

9

Colonel Neil Brittan

/ / /

In 1940, before the war, my parents proudly decorated the largest wall in the front parlor of our Cartagena plantation house with an Oklahoma A&M pennant that spanned the length of the room. It was that orange and black pennant that brought Neil Brittan into our lives for a few hours.

We were still living on the beach after Pearl Harbor, but Dad was about to move us to a more secure place near the high jungle because Japanese gunboats were shelling populated areas along the coast.

One afternoon, all four of us were away from home on some errand for an hour or so and when we returned we were met by one of our house-boys, who informed us we had a visitor. I rather imagine that news may have caused my parents some anxiety but the servant did not seem frightened by the stranger's presence, so we proceeded into the house. Standing in our living room was a tall, very rangy Caucasian man wearing khakis without military insignia, although his combat boots gave away the fact that he was surely an American soldier. He had shaggy reddish-brown hair and a startlingly red beard.

The man introduced himself as Neil Brittan, a colonel in the U.S. Army who was sent south to investigate the possibility of salvaging the munitions cargo on the sunken USS *Panay* in Miracalum Bay. Stationed with American troops on the neighboring island, the ship's namesake Panay, in the city of Iloilo, Brittan was on a last-resort mission to see if any of the badly needed military supplies on the ship could be recovered to relieve the beleaguered troops on Luzon.

"I was walking through the village," Colonel Brittan said. "Someone told me an American lived here so I came up to your house. Your doors and windows were open, and I saw an Oklahoma A&M pennant on your wall. I couldn't believe it. That's where I went to college. I'm an Aggie grad myself. I grew up in Waukomis, Oklahoma."

Startled, my mother looked more closely at the man. "Are you Rena Penn's husband?" she asked. Questioningly, he nodded.

Mother began to laugh and cry at the same time. "You're the Neil Brittan I went to college with at A&M in 1931!"

The colonel was as astounded as she was and for a moment he couldn't speak. "You know my wife?" he said.

"Yes, I know your wife," my mother said. "Rena Penn and I had several classes together. She teaches art in the home economics department, doesn't she?"

Colonel Brittan sank back into a chair. He was very tired. His eyes were red-rimmed, his face haggard, his whole body slumped in fatigue.

"Have you eaten?" said my father. "Let us get you some food."

"Your servants gave me tea and cookies," Colonel Brittan said. "They have been very kind."

My mother was rummaging in the bookshelves for her 1931 college yearbook.

"Here she is," said Mother. "Here's Rena and here I am, and look—there's you!"

He rubbed his eyes wearily with a sunburned hand. "I couldn't believe it," he said. "I thought I was hallucinating when I looked into your front room and saw that A&M pennant on the wall."

We invited Colonel Brittan to stay for supper and spend the night. After a hot bath and a fine meal, he was shown to the guest room, where he stretched out on a bed for the first rest and unworried sleep he had had in weeks.

Next morning at breakfast, my parents and Brittan continued their reminiscing about mutual friends, college experiences, and Oklahoma ties. But the reality of the present couldn't be put aside and the conversation turned to what was happening in the war.

"If things continue to be bad and the fighting ends in the north, we want you to come here, Colonel Brittan," my father said. "We will organize a guerrilla force and we will continue to fight the Japs. We will not let them overrun this country and we will not be subjugated."

"No," the colonel said. "If Luzon falls, and Iloilo falls, there's an American unit in Mindanao, headed up by a mining engineer named Fertig. I know him. He's from Colorado. He's a good military man and I understand he has some equipment and some men. Some are his own and some are escapees from Manila. If our unit in Panay is forced to surrender, I will join up with Fertig in Mindanao."

"But how will you get there?" said my mother. "Mindanao is the farthest island south. How will you get across the water?"

"I'll get there," said Colonel Brittan. "I'll get there. I've had a lot of help from the Filipinos. They've found me boats, they've guided me from village to village, they've given me food. I can get there, eventually."

"Colonel Brittan," my father said, "The farther south you travel, the fewer people you'll find who speak English. You've only been in the Philippines a short while. You know so little of the language, so little of the country. You look unmistakably American. You tower over us with your height, your beard is red, you have blue eyes. The Japanese are paying bounty for men like you, American officers. The country people gossip, and word of you will spread faster than you can travel."

My father continued: "Your chances of getting through are very slim. You cannot disguise your American appearance and you have no experience in the jungle. You can't communicate in the Visayan language and its various dialects that change almost from barrio to barrio."

Now my father was pleading: "Our people will not betray you if you stay here. They are fighters themselves and they will welcome your leadership and your military skill. They need an American colonel like you to inspire them and demonstrate that the United States has not written off the Philippines completely."

My father kept on, desperately trying to convince the colonel of the folly of his fall-back plan. "If you do get to Moro country—and Mindanao is Moro, Moslem—you will be in greater danger than you have ever been. The Moslems do not like Americans. They do not like anyone from outside their culture, their religion. They call themselves Filipinos, but they kill Christian Filipinos as a religious obligation. And they hate Americans even more."

Colonel Brittan would not be dissuaded. His first duty as a soldier was to fight under the flag of the United States, and if his own unit surrendered he was determined to go to Mindanao, from where General MacArthur had gone to Australia shortly before.

The colonel left Cartagena that morning, walking south with two or three guerrilla guides that my father provided. They carried baskets of food my mother prepared for his journey. We never saw him again.

Among the first people my mother contacted after we came to Oklahoma in 1945 was Rena Penn Brittan. We went to her office in the home economics art department at Oklahoma A&M in Stillwater. Mrs. Brittan had a

A Letter to My Father

pile of Associated Press wire photos on her desk. The pictures were all of American prisoners of war rescued in the Philippines, in Japan, and in Manchuria. The men were gaunt, hollow-eyed, clearly the victims of unspeakable suffering.

Mrs. Brittan showed the pictures to my mother. "I thought, since you were the last one to see him, that you might be able to recognize him in a picture," she said. "This one here—he has Neil's eyes but I don't think he's as tall. And here, this man has Neil's build, square shoulders, long arms, fairly large hands. Does he look familiar? Did he look like that when you saw him?"

My mother looked at the pictures with sadness, her heart breaking. How could she offer hope, or destroy hope, when she survived? How could my mother say aloud what she wanted so much to say: "Oh Rena, if only he had listened to us. If only he had stayed with us on Negros. He would have been safe and could have come home."

But that would have been conjecture. Colonel Brittan did what he had to do. If he had stayed on Negros, who is to say that he would have lived to come home? For four years, we walked through the shadow of death. The chances were even that none of us would come home.

Colonel Brittan's son, Oklahoma film director Shawnee Brittan, made a documentary of his father's story. Although Nelson Brittan (he changed his birth name to Shawnee when he began working in the film industry) and I attended A&M at almost the same time, we had never compared notes about our World War II connection. It was not until I learned of the film project, *Sleep My Sons*, that Shawnee Brittan and I got together and I at last found out what had happened to his father. My husband and I were invited to the gala premiere of the documentary in 1996.

Nelson Brittan has spent his adult life tracing his father's fate after the fall of the Philippines. Colonel Brittan made it to Mindanao and reported to the last remnant of the United States Armed Forces in the Far East still

62

on duty in the Philippines. The unit held out, fighting with Filipino guerrilleros, but some of its soldiers were captured and sent to prison camp in Luzon. When the war turned into disaster for Japan in 1944, American prisoners of war were shipped to Japan and Japanese-occupied Manchuria to work in labor camps and held as hostages in the eventuality that U.S. forces invaded the Japanese homeland.

Shawnee Brittan found his father's name on the manifest of the *Arisan Maru,* one of the Japanese vessels that have come to be known as "hell ships." Loaded with American and Filipino POWs, the unmarked *Arisan Maru* was bombed by U.S. airplanes off the coast of Luzon on October 24, 1944. Neil Brittan perished, along with all but seven of his comrades.

How I wish now that, when we were young, I could have told Shawnee Brittan and his sister, Lamoyne, "Your father was a brave man. A hero. Be proud. And I am grateful."

A Letter from My Father

Isabella, Occ. Negros

April 16, 1942

Darling & Kiddies:

We are back again here. Stayed up in the mountains for two days then came down here.

Honey, I wish I could see all of you once more. The present situation is very, very serious after the capture of Bataan. However, the Ilocos Provinces are still fighting the Japanese up there.

Honey dear, I depend on you to do the most safest way for the children and yourself especially. May we all [be] fortunate to meet again. Hope for the best. Be calm, dear. Remember your two children. Move, act wisely for your safety. Honey, stay in the mountain as soon as you hear that the Japs has already landed in this Province. Do not give them any chance to see you. Take plenty on the mountain.

Slaughter one of the young vaca and make tapa for your provision. Honey dear, be very careful always.

The plan for fighting the Japanese in this province if and when they come is the guerrilla warfare. No chance except this as we have no bomber[s] here. We do not know why no aid has come until now. Talking and talking but no results. Oh honey, why [is the] U.S.A. letting us suffer here? I know in the long run the Japs are bound to lose but dear, what shall we do when we are all gone?

Darling, you know I am insured and it is up to [you] to dig it up in case any serious thing may happen to me in this struggle for our country. Honey dear, go back to the States with the children in case I do not return to you. However, pray for our Jesus Christ for my safety to return to you. Dear, don't let the Japs see you. Hide as much as you can inside the forest. You have plenty of hiding place out there and so do all you can.

Now dear Helen Judy and Mang, let me stop this time. I will always write you whenever I can. Pray for the Lord for our safety. Helen be a good girl; same to you Judy. Tell Mang that all of you should hide on the mountain when Japanese is now in this province. They are fighting heavily in Cebu at this time.

Kisses to you, Helen, Judy and Mang. *

> *Daddy*

*Author's note: *Mang* is a diminutive for *Mamang*, the Visayan equivalent of "Mommy."

10

The First Hideout

/ / /

In April 1942, when we visited Dad at the army camp in north Negros, he and
Mother decided it was time for us to move away from the beach. We left
our house with its pillared veranda and moved to a place Mom named
Evac, an abbreviation for "evacuation." It was at the edge of the jungle, far
from populated settlements and off the main trail of travel. One of Mother's
household helpers came with us to take care of my brother and me so
Mom could manage the plantation in Dad's absence. In a letter she hoped
someday to mail to her family, Mom wrote, "I continued to go to the
office [in Cartagena] every day until the Province was surrendered but
after that, I remained in hiding. Mr. Asibal [the farm overseer], being
Filipino, was not in so much danger as I, so he assumed the entire work.
Our tenants were convinced that so long as the enemy did not station
forces in our immediate vicinity, they should be working to produce food,

so our rice fields are all planted. In the occupied portions of the Province, little farm work was being done."

Having left the wood-burning range in the kitchen of the Cartagena house, Mother and Estrella, our helper, cooked in *kalans* (clay pots) and a cast-iron skillet over an open wood fire. They washed dishes in scalding hot water in a tin dishpan on a crude wooden table. We still had a few china dishes and some knives, forks, and spoons, and we had regular meals—breakfast, lunch, and dinner—preserving the dignity of a normal household schedule. Evac was in a clearing on a hillside, unobstructed by big trees or rocks, so Mother was able to start a flock of laying hens; she even took up pig-farming on a small scale. She sent Estrella down to the local farmers' market on the beach every Saturday with eggs, live fryers, stewing hens, and piglets to sell or trade for fish, shrimp, clams, occasionally raw sugar known as muscovado, and substitute coffee made of ground roasted corn and chicory. We had our own truck garden that provided vegetables for our daily diet and Mother had access to plenty of rice from the tenant farmers. We did not lack for food—even in the dark and terrifying months to come, I don't remember ever going to bed hungry. Such was my mother and father's determination to see that we would not be deprived of proper nutrition.

With that in mind, Mother quietly began to learn to cook with ingredients she was not familiar with, especially those that grew wild. She established trade with the farm women who lived in the foothills and, in the letter she hoped someday to send to her family in the States, she wrote, "We are fortunate to have one neighbor family who plants quite a good variety of vegetables [that we didn't have in our own garden] and they are so liberal with them. They will never accept money for anything . . . but of course we have been able to reciprocate in [other] ways."

Mom also made friends with the very shy women of the *kaingin*, the nomads who roamed the mountains, planting patches of dry-land rice on the small high meadows. The men spear-hunted birds and wild boar, and the families lived in temporary shelters of nipa and bamboo until the year's supply of rice was harvested, then they packed up and moved on to other sites. They rarely were in contact with other than their own clan; they were a gentle people and bothered no one. Mother gained their confidence when she was close enough, a few times, to offer them something nice, like a bit of ribbon or a roasted sweet potato or a few lumps of brown sugar. When she was able to provide help for a sick child or show them how to use bar soap to wash their clothes, the *kaingin* women were forever grateful and became her ally. They showed her where to select edible tree mushrooms, find jungle squash vines and wild spinach, pick cashew fruit for the nuts, dig the tenderest, most delectable bamboo shoots, and make tea out of native herbs and blossoms.

At the same time, my brother learned to catch fresh-water shrimp and fish in the mountain streams. Although he was just six years old when the war began, he became a proficient weaver of basket shrimp traps of bamboo and rattan, and he learned how to place them in the narrowest channels so the shrimp were forced to swim into the trap. It was Jorge J.'s trapping talent that provided us with protein after it became too dangerous to send someone to the beach for seafood. Later on, when we were on the march, we often depended solely on my little brother to bring in the evening's dinner.

Even before the war started, our mother was very concerned that we might not have milk to drink. There were no dairy cows on the island, therefore, we used canned and powdered milk for drinking and cooking. Mother bought it by the case, along with other staples, up north and brought it home so we usually had several months' supply. But with the prospect of war looming, Mother's first priority was to insure that we would have an alternate source of milk. Thus began what I remember as the Episode of the Goat.

Goats were a fairly common livestock on the island. They were raised for meat, not for milk, but we never had goat meat on our table. My father didn't like the taste of goat meat, and my mother, coming from beef country, had the same disdain for it that she had for lamb. However, she had grown up in Ellis County milking cows, so she knew she could learn to milk a goat.

There was a tenant on the plantation, Gregorio, who kept a herd of fine healthy-looking goats. One day when he was at our house conferring on some kind of rice-farm business, my mother opened negotiations with him for the purchase of a goat. She did not want an adult nanny; she preferred a weaner vixen that she could raise herself to make sure the goat would not be a carrier of disease. 'Gorio assured Mother enthusiastically that even as he spoke there was a female goat in his flock about to kid—or whatever it is goats do when they give birth. Mother was delighted. She gave 'Gorio a two-peso deposit and was promised a baby goat shortly.

A week or so went by. 'Gorio came and went several times, each time apologizing to my mother for the lateness of his pregnant goat's delivery. My mother became impatient. The last case of evaporated milk was nearly used up and it was becoming apparent that we would have to flee into the hills before the supply lines to outside groceries opened up again. Mother gave 'Gorio another peso, hoping to speed up his goat's gestation.

The next time or two that 'Gorio came around, Mother had the distinct impression he was avoiding her. Then she became upset and one day she trapped 'Gorio as he was obviously sneaking away. She told him she had waited long enough. She threatened him with a lawsuit to recover her cash deposit with interest and punitive damages. How she intended to accomplish that, I can't explain. We didn't have a civil court in southern Negros to speak of, even in peacetime. Nevertheless, my mother laid it on poor 'Gorio. She demanded he produce the baby goat he had contracted to sell her in a fair and legal business agreement. My mother's fury was more than 'Gorio could handle. After much shuffling of feet and with downcast eyes, he finally confessed.

This all took place during the time that Dad was at home every few days. It seems he did not want the goat, milk or no milk. He disliked goats because of their smell, their silly bleat, and the way they jumped around. They ate the leaves and bark off of trees, ultimately destroying them, which in my father's mind was a crime against nature. Most of all, he was repulsed by the thought of eating food prepared with goat's milk and he couldn't bear the possibility of watching his children drink goat's milk at his table.

'Gorio had come upon a perfect scam, a little shakedown that was more profitable than selling a goat. He timed each trip to our house when he was certain Dad was at home. When 'Gorio came to the house to announce the arrival of Mother's kid, my father paid him off with twenty centavos to go away. It turned into a cash cow—or cash goat—for 'Gorio. No wonder he was showing up once or twice a week.

Mother ultimately acquired what by then was a very expensive goat. To make amends, 'Gorio threw in the use of the mother goat for milking purposes until the female kid reached the age of motherhood. My father resigned himself to living on a goat farm and by the time we moved to Evac, we had a whole herd of goats. My brother and I loved them; they were even better pets than our dogs, Buster and Wainwright. Mother trained the nannies to jump up and stand still on a platform she built with the help of one of the guerrilleros. It was kitchen-cabinet height, so she didn't have to lie on her stomach to milk.

We drank goat milk morning and night. It was thin and watery and warm; we had no refrigeration so we drank the milk al fresco and it certainly had a goaty flavor, but it was milk, nonetheless. Mom considered it worth all the trouble she had gone through for us to have a couple of cups of milk every day. She mixed a little cocoa in my brother's serving because it was the only way he would drink milk from any source; at that time she still had some cans of Hershey's.

When we had to leave Evac and go into total concealment in the jungle, we gave the goats to 'Gorio. Mother didn't charge him; 'Gorio had redeemed himself. They were a gift for his friendship. I have not drunk goat milk since that time in 1942. But I adore feta cheese and now when I eat it, I think about the Episode of the Goat.

11

A Book of Matches
and an Apple

/ / /

We lived in our first evacuation home until after the Japanese occupied northern Negros. My father commanded a quartermaster unit responsible for supplying the island's guerrilla troops. Because of his familiarity with the farms and warehouses of southern Negros, and his good relationships with the farmers and local officials, he was the most likely and best-trained officer to create a supply line. It meant that we—Jorge J., Mother and I, and one or two trusted guerrillero-household assistants—were alone for days or weeks at a time. My father always had a "runner" who kept him in contact with us, and Dad himself came home nearly every week or two to make sure we were all right and to see to it that we had food and other supplies.

Many people who have known me since the war assume Dad was away from us for three years because that's how they perceive a soldier in battle. It has been hard to explain that we were actually in a war zone as much as he, most of the time, although Dad made it a point, whenever possible, to have his troop encampment in the opposite direction so as not to draw even more danger upon us. Although we were directly under fire only once during those years, Mother, Jorge J., and I were often within walking distance of firefights.

The south of Negros had no particular military importance, except for its food supply, in the first year of the war, and the enemy didn't find it necessary to put a permanent troop deployment in the area. But, to put it mildly, the Japanese were annoyed that my mother, an American, and my father, an officer in the United States Army, were insubordinately refusing to turn themselves in. I suppose they banked on our inability to endure the primitive living conditions in the jungle and that, sooner or later, we would trade in for the "security" of a concentration camp. They underestimated my parents.

We knew that eventually enemy soldiers would come looking for us. My parents moved our household deeper into the mountains, to a place we named Sunny Slope. The house we lived in there was smaller and less convenient than our first Evac, but it was clean and it sheltered us from the torrential jungle rains so we settled into relative comfort. We had to make do without Mother's garden because there was so little sunshine and we had to say goodbye to the goats and our two dogs. It was during this time that I began reading my mother's college literature textbooks in earnest, and writing fantasies of my own.

It was also during this time that we experienced a scourge of locusts. It's hard to describe how destructive those little creatures were. They swarmed in one afternoon and blanketed the small grassy meadow just down the hill from our house, in a cloud so dense it blocked the sun. The meadow was turned into open dirt in less than an hour. Some of the smaller saplings at the edge of the jungle were literally defoliated as if they'd undergone a killing hailstorm. Fortunately, our nipa-thatched hut was sheltered by the first row of big jungle trees or we might have found ourselves roofless.

74

Mother had read of the scourges of locusts in Biblical times but this onslaught was surreal, something before which we were truly helpless.

We feared that the rice fields and kitchen gardens, banana groves, and pasture lands in the valley would be decimated, and we later learned that many of them were destroyed before the locusts ate their fill and departed. But people were not totally without recourse. We watched our two young guerrilleros rush into the insect swarm with gunny sacks and other make-shift trapping devices to trap locusts by the basketful. Bringing the catch into the house, the young men showed my mother how to prepare the critters for dinner. Locusts may not sound palatable to Western tastes but they were a providential source of food—probably loaded with protein and calcium—that came from the sky unannounced, unbidden, and dreaded but nonetheless usefully contributing to the human food supply. Roasted and salted, the locusts had a keeping quality that made them safely edible for some time, as convenient as being flash-frozen or dehydrated. It must have taken a great measure of my mother's intestinal fortitude to accept locusts as a decent form of human nutrition but in this instance she was flexible, and Jorge J. and I had no compunctions about enjoying the nutty, crunchy texture and flavor of locusts. I think Mother tasted a few just to prove she wasn't a wimp, but I doubt she relished them as much as we did.

The guerrilla resistance in the Visayas was energized when my father's unit decided to salvage the USS *Panay* in Miracalum Bay. The ship had been bound for Corregidor in January of 1942 with ammunition and supplies desperately needed by the beleaguered Filipino and U.S. troops in what would be their last stand to save the Philippines from Japanese occupation. Unaccompanied by air or naval escorts, the *Panay* was attempting to make its way north under cover of nighttime, seeking concealment during daylight in the deep bays of the inner islands. The enemy discovered the *Panay*'s location when it was lying over on the southern end of Negros. Japanese bombers were dispatched to sink it.

There was no way to save the USS *Panay* from sinking but several months later my father, as quartermaster of the Negros guerrillas, decided to salvage the ship, to bring up whatever precious guns and ammunition could be retrieved for the resistance to the Japanese occupation. Salvage divers, as such, were not available, so my father recruited pearl divers, men and women who used no underwater breathing equipment, no air hoses or tanks or underwater lights, to go deep into the ocean for incredible lengths of time. The divers slipped naked into the sea, far down into its depths, and hitched ropes to wooden crates packed with bullets, grenades, and other explosives. The crates were pulled up and hauled to shore on bancas.

It was an exhilarating and encouraging beginning for the citizen soldiers of the guerrilla resistance. Now they had the means to fight, a supply depot, meager though it was and perhaps never very effective after its months-long settling in sea water. For my dad and his soldiers, however, the load of munitions on the sunken *Panay* was far more potent than bamboo staves and primitive slingshots and bolos.

On December 27, 1942, a real ray of hope arose for the beleaguered little army on Negros. At dawn a platoon of my father's soldiers was walking along the beach to continue the USS *Panay* salvage project when they met three men whom none of them knew. Although the men were not in uniform, the guerrilla farmers and teenage boys immediately recognized the strangers as military. Some of the guerrilleros spoke of having seen, or thinking they had seen, in the early morning, the outline of a submarine on the surface of the horizon, but in the predawn mist it quickly disappeared beneath the sea. The three strangers were immediately taken prisoner by the guerrilleros, who were waiting for their commander, my father, to arrive.

The captives spoke a Filipino language that none of the guerrilleros could understand, nor could the strangers understand the Visayan language of southern Negros. The captives were searched, disarmed, and tied with hemp rope to coconut trees. When shortly thereafter, my father arrived, he at once recognized the language the strangers spoke.

"We are here, sir, to work with a crew of coconut pickers," said one of the three men. "We've come from Cebu and we will join our crew this afternoon."

My father noted that the coconut-picker story was fraught with inaccuracies. The man spoke Tagalog, a language no Cebuano would use in those years. Furthermore, all three men had straight white teeth, unstained by beetlenut juice. Although they were barefoot, they didn't have splayed-out toes from years of climbing the trunks of coconut trees. My father was reluctant to contradict these men as they could surely be collaborators, sent by the Japanese into the hinterlands to gather information and report on guerrilla troop strength.

As the sun came up and lighted the men's faces, my father felt a shock of recognition. The spokesman for the three strangers was someone he recognized, a man whose picture had been published on the front page of one of the last issues of the *Manila Daily Bulletin* in December 1941. In that picture, my father remembered, the man wore a U.S. Army Air Corps uniform and he was being lauded for shooting down the most Japanese airplanes during the battle to save Manila.

My father took the man aside and saluted. "Welcome to Negros, General Villamor," he said in a soft voice.

"Not quite, Captain," said the stranger. "I'm Major Villamor. Jess Villamor. You are now a guerrillero?"

"Yes," my father said. "I command these troops."

Major Jesus Villamor, a fighter pilot in the U.S. Army Air Corps who accompanied Douglas MacArthur to Australia early in 1942, had volunteered to go back to the Philippines less than a year later to evaluate the guerrilla movement, provide it with supplies, and prepare the islands for liberation.

Major Villamor had with him two subordinates, Lieutenant del Rosario, a signal corpsman, and Lieutenant Reyes. All served in the U.S. Army under orders from General MacArthur.

Villamor's special force, which at that time we referred to as "the commandos," had what may have been the most important mission in the liberation of the Philippines. For almost a year, MacArthur had been cut off from the men and women he had left behind in Bata-an and Corregidor. There was sporadic radio contact but nothing that could be verified about a resistance effort. Nor was there any intelligence on how to contact the leaders of a resistance movement if it existed.

Jesus Villamor, thirty, was brilliantly educated in the Philippines, and after finishing college, he learned to be a fighter pilot at a U.S. training base in Texas. In the days following Pearl Harbor, Villamor was one of the few Filipino airmen still flying. Jess, with nerves of steel, performed some of the most dangerous solo missions during the short weeks before the Philippines surrendered. He was decorated with the Distinguished Service Cross by the United States.

General MacArthur, mapping out his determined return to the Philippines, chose Jess Villamor and Lieutenant del Rosario and Lieutenant Reyes to go back into the Japanese-held territory of the Philippines. The three officers went aboard the submarine USS *Gudgeon* disguised as mess boys to travel underwater through Japanese sea lanes, ultimately to Cartagena Bay. There they were off-loaded with a rubber raft and a stack of small wooden boxes, along with the submarine captain's prayerful blessing for their safety.

Villamor, del Rosario, and Reyes inflated the raft and paddled it to the beach, and while it was still dark, hurriedly dug a deep hole in the sand some distance beyond the high tide line and buried the boxes and the deflated raft. Then the three set out to find some locals so they could assess the prevailing conditions.

I note here that it seems no one at USAFFE headquarters in Australia thought to include a Negros Visayan speaker in the intelligence group. In its defense, however, the commando team was to land on the island of Leyte, but was diverted to Negros after the submarine was underway.

(There's a common opinion that all Filipinos speak Tagalog, and perhaps now they do because it is the official language. I know Filipinos who still don't speak Tagalog and never intend to because they are proud of their provincial heritage. So much for "official" language.)

And so it was that my father and mother became an integral part of the World War II liberation of the Philippines.

The day after the commandos landed at Cartagena, two guerrilleros appeared at our Sunny Slope hideout up in the hills, miles from the beach. As was customary in the transportation of packages and freight, the young men carried two or three big baskets strapped on a pair of poles across their shoulders.

My brother and I took little notice of the deliveries, expecting the baskets to contain perhaps some foraged canned goods or a bolt of cotton fabric found in an abandoned tailoring shop. My mother had the carriers bring the freight into our "kitchen" and she began opening the baskets. I heard her yell out in surprise. She held up a bright red tin box and my brother and I rushed to see what was in it.

As she pried open the cover, the three of us leaned forward to peer inside. Mother reached into the tin box and as her hand emerged we gasped. She was holding a large shiny red Delicious apple. Jorge J. and I had only faint memories of having seen apples before but we knew what they were and that they were grown in the United States. Then Mother reached into the tin box again and this time she brought out a fistful of hard candy,

Christmas candy—striped peppermints, butterballs, red-hots, raspberry drops, lemon drops, and candy canes. Farther down in the box, in separate wrappings were animal crackers, soda crackers, chocolate cookies, and of all things, something I'd never seen before—book matches. On their covers were printed the words, "I Shall Return."

12

The Coming of
Major Villamor

/ / /

Hours later, my father and the three officers he had "captured" showed up at Sunny Slope, our foothill hideout. We were beside ourselves with joy. These brave men who came to us from Australia were warm and funny, full of energy and enthusiasm. They spoke a beautiful, slang-filled American language that even my mother sometimes had trouble understanding. Most of all, they brought us news and hope. They told us about General MacArthur's military recuperation in Australia, about the mobilization in the United States, about the naval campaigns and air missions on the long road back to the Philippines. After a year of isolation following Pearl Harbor and MacArthur's retreat, my parents finally had a little knowledge of what was happening in the war that transversed the world.

Major Jesus Villamor was the most glamorous man I have ever known. He was a pilot, a fighter pilot. He shot down a record number of Japanese aircraft in the battle before the fall of Manila, earning the U.S. Air Force's highest commendation. But he was soft-spoken, unassuming, not one to assert himself over others. My brother and I could hardly breathe in his presence. He introduced himself to my parents as "Jess," but they could never bring themselves to call him anything but "the Major." Jorge J. and I were instructed to call him "Major" and never say his real name aloud, even among the guerrilleros. It was the most important secret we had to keep during the war.

My father brought in his troop of enlisted men, whom I now think of as the world's quintessential multi-tasking workers, second only to the Oklahoma sodbusters of 1887. Within a day or two, the guerrilleros built a shed next to our home, where the commandos set up a communications center and sleeping quarters for the three officers. The communications center was always padlocked when Lieutenant del Rosario wasn't in it.

The three took their meals at my mother's table, to their delight and Mother's joy. The men offered to share their field rations but we all preferred to eat fresh food. I recall that when one of the officers came down with a fever, Major Villamor gave Mom his medical kit and she dosed the ailing commando with whatever form of medicine was issued by the military in 1943. The sick one became well soon, but I attribute his quick recovery to Mama's chicken soup.

Lieutenant del Rosario was the radioman. He was a chubby, happy man who dearly loved us. One night while he was on the radio, listening to whatever was going over the airwaves, he motioned me over as I watched him. He took his earphones off and placed them on my head. I listened hard and, very faintly, I heard the sound of music and a female voice singing, "You'll never know just how much I miss you. You'll never know just how much I care."

For me, it was a mesmerizing experience. Nowhere in my memory now is there a melody as haunting as that song, "You'll Never Know."

Lieutenant Reyes, a charmer, was the youngest of the three officers. Whatever his specialty was, I think he was the killer. He was small and lithe and gloriously handsome and very dark. He was sent along, I believe, to protect Lieutenant del Rosario, who was an extremely valuable signal corpsman, and Major Villamor, probably the Philippines' most important war hero.

Although it was in a sense a mission of mercy, the Villamor operation brought us fully into the war. The radio transmitter installation was almost inside our house. It took only a few weeks for the Japanese to trace its location. Then the commandos knew they had to move on. Having established contact with my father's south Negros guerrilla troops, Major Villamor went north and on to other islands to carry out his mission. But before he left us, he tried to persuade my mother to take my brother and me with her to Australia by submarine.

U.S. Navy submarines were coming into the Philippines loaded with military supplies and returning to Darwin with plenty of passenger space. I am sure Mother and Dad discussed the invitation thoroughly but when the decision was made, our mother's will prevailed.

She turned Major Villamor down. She refused to leave my father and, I think, she didn't want to leave the Philippines for a foreign land—Australia—in which she was a stranger. Mother knew the Philippines, where she had lived for ten years. She knew the good people, so much like her own. She couldn't leave them now, not when there was hope that they would make it through this horrible war, that they would see their own country become independent and self-sufficient, that there would be vindication, eventually, for her teachings and my father's teaching, that good food and clean water and happy reading for children, and vocational opportunity for young adults, would one day make the Philippines a true land of freedom, a horizon opening on a more peaceful world.

My mother never told me that there were submarine-loads of Americans and Filipino Americans who took Major Villamor's humanitarian offer, who made the harrowing trip underwater to Australia, and eventually to the United States in 1943. I learned of it after I was an adult, reading of the exodus in postwar accounts. Eventually, some of the rescued returned to the Philippines and resumed their jobs as teachers and doctors and missionaries and agricultural industrialists. Iva Madamba chose to stay in the Philippines through the long haul till war's end, perhaps the last American to choose voluntarily to see it through on the island of Negros.

After the war, from 1947 through the early 1960s, while my father worked in the United Nations and then the U.S. Agency for International Development, he visited Jess Villamor in Washington, D.C., whenever he was in that city. Villamor was in the Philippine diplomatic delegation with Ambassador Carlos Romulo, another of my father's friends in high international circles. I never saw Major Villamor again after he left the wartime encampment we called Sunny Slope. Twenty-some years later, I met someone in Northern California who told me that he and his wife had been neighbors of Jess Villamor and his family in the Washington apartment complex where they lived. The Villamors were the godparents of his child.

Such is the eerie stuff of coincidence in my life's journey.

Recently, while I was going through a box of my dad's papers that Jorge J. gave me, I found this letter.

In The Field
May 4th, 1943

My Dear Capt. Madamba:

Its really a long time snce we last see each other. I hope that everyone in the family are doing alright. My kindest thoughts to the Mrs., Helen and Judy. Please remind me to them.

In leaving this island where everyone was so kind and thoughtful, it is with a heavy heart that I say adieu, but wherever I may be, my thoughts and prayers will be always for those, who in my short stay here, were so kind to me.

Wish you and the mrs. all the happiness in this world and here's hoping we may meet again very soon.

Thanking you again for everything you have done for me.

I remain,

Sincerely yours,

(sgd) J. del Rosario

J. del Rosario

2nd Lt. S.C.

A.U.S.

13

The Abyss of Danger

/ / /

Within days after Major Villamor's team left Sunny Slope, the Japanese established a garrison in Cartagena, our village on the beach. They probably quartered themselves in our plantation house. They were determined to root out the burgeoning guerrilla effort, now encouraged and supplied directly from U.S. forces in Australia. But their main target was my father because he was the first United States Army officer to be contacted by MacArthur's special force, and because he headed up the supply line for the rest of the island. Furthermore, and perhaps most galling of all, my father's wife was an American woman who was every bit as tenacious as he. That they had two children to protect made our holdout even more enticing; the Japanese knew they held a trump card if ever we were to fall into their hands.

It was midspring of 1943 when we picked up our evacuation kits and hiked into the high trees, where we could see the sun only at its zenith, and boulders piled one upon the other concealed us.

My brother and I were admonished by our mother not to cry, not to quarrel, not to laugh out loud. Sounds of voices carry far through the jungle. We whispered, even when we fell and scraped our knees, or when we had earaches or toothaches, which was often for me, and when we were angry and disagreeable. It amazes me now that Mother had the fortitude to keep two children quiet when our natural inclination was to be boisterous and active and high-spirited. Before we went into the jungle, I was given to throwing vehement temper tantrums when I didn't get my way. I held my breath and dashed myself on the floor, kicking and screaming. I remember once, early in my childhood, when Mother was so fed up with my hysterical behavior she poured a bucket of cold water over my head. I'm sure it calmed me down.

Somehow, Mother was able to make me understand that our lives were at stake, that out among the rocks and in the vines and up in the mammoth trees there might be enemy soldiers, who had bayonets fixed on their rifles, ready to run us through if they found us. But she convinced us in a way that we didn't live every moment cowering in fear and trembling. She made us realize what our responsibility was for our own safety and her safety, as well as the safety of the guerrilleros who were looking after us. It was then, I think, that I learned to swallow my anger, my insecurity, my pain and anxiety.

From time to time, our mother had to punish us for misbehaving, as children will under any circumstances. She could still threaten us with a switch, reminding us first that we couldn't yelp, or she could make us stand in "a corner"—which was at the base of a tree or behind a particular rock pile. But generally, I think, our discipline problems were minimal. I spent most of my daylight hours reading and Jorge J. was occupied making shrimp traps and setting them in the streams. The tedium was surely harder on her than it was on us, although she most certainly had a lot on her mind during those months of life-or-death uncertainty.

We slept in shelters that consisted of nipa-thatched sheds over bamboo platforms built a foot or so above the ground to keep us dry. Mother cooked on a campfire that would do a Boy Scout proud—a ring of stones set level on the ground for the rice pot and whatever stir-fry was on the menu for the day. We gathered wood in the forest for the cooking fire, hoping it wasn't too wet to burn. We ate our meals from coconut shell halves that had been scrubbed out and polished to a lovely sheen. We had no forks, no table knives, and only two or three serving-size spoons, so we used our fingers to scoop rice and shrimp and wild vegetables into our mouths. Most of the time there was no sugar for any sort of dessert or sweet between-meal snacks. Mom wanted us to drink a kind of wild camphor tea that she said was good for us. I recall that it tasted like Mentholatum; I would not drink it today. For coffee, Mother roasted dried corn and ground it in a small hand-grinder that she managed to pack along with the few cooking utensils our helpers could carry. Occasionally, she was able to barter for chicory from a friendly guerrillero passing through. Mixed with the ground corn, it made a fair substitute for coffee.

The young boys that my dad stationed to stay with us camped nearby. One of their jobs was to pound rice in a hollow log mortar with wooden pestles shaped like elongated baseball bats. The pounding had a soothing rhythm, set according to the number of pounders. It separated the inner grains of rice from their hulls. The first stage of pounding produced brown rice, which Mother, ever the dietician, considered most healthy and nutritious. However our dad was a picky eater. When he was home, Mother let the helpers pound longer, until the rice was polished white.

At night, we had for a while a Coleman pump lantern fueled with kerosene. However, it was a dangerously bright light and Mother was probably relieved when its last mantle disintegrated, although it meant we couldn't read after sundown. From that time on, we relied on coconut shells and coconut oil with floating cotton wicks, which we made from our precious few rags. That provided us with illumination that was easily doused and we lighted those only when it was absolutely necessary. To my knowledge, the Japanese didn't often foray in the dark where they were as vulnerable as we were. Guerrilla soldiers loved to find them in situations where they could be attacked at a disadvantage.

It was never cold in the Philippine jungle. When the sun set—and it set quite early in that equatorial latitude—the temperature changed very little. I owned two or three changes of clothes, a dress, a jumper, and a blouse that I had when the war started in 1941, and not much more. Mother was a great seamstress and, when she could trade for a yard or so of fabric, she hand-sewed shirts and pants for Jorge, and pinafores for me. We slept in the same clothes we wore during the day, provided they were clean. Our mother scrubbed our laundry in the streams, using whatever soap she had hoarded or made when she could find pork fat to mix with ash lye. We had no need of bed linens (we had no beds) and we bathed in the river and air-dried ourselves without towels.

Mother valiantly tried to look after our dental health. She mashed the ends of green twigs for us to use as toothbrushes, dipped in sea salt as a substitute for tooth paste. It is wonderful that my brother has been a practicing dentist for forty years and his teeth are as straight, sound, and white as those of a modern teenager who has all the benefits of twenty-first-century orthodontia.

You ask: "Where did you go to the bathroom?" My answer is, "Out back." Each time we stopped in a new hideout, Mother scoped out the lay of the land and the nearest water source. She directed us to use a specific area that was below the flow of the stream, well screened by bushes and far enough away from our living space to avoid flies. Before we went into the jungle we had a Sears Roebuck catalog to use for toilet tissue but we couldn't use it when we were on the run as it would have left an obvious trail for a Japanese search party to follow. From then on, we had to resort to leaves—and here again, my cautious mother tested them to make sure they were not some tropical form of poison oak.

We vacated each hideout when my father determined that the Japanese were getting too close to our location. Because there were flyers posted in the villages and along the main trails offering a ransom for our capture, Dad was constantly on the alert for any rumor of our whereabouts. For a time, the word was out that our mother had died of malaria—and that gave us a measure of safety as the enemy relaxed its search for her. Within a month or two, the Japanese learned that she was very much alive—and so we were off again, to a hiding place farther into the hills.

When Dad deemed it too dangerous for us to stay where we were, he would come "home" to lead us to a new campsite deeper into the rain-forest and farther up the Cordillera mountain range that formed the spine of Negros Island. Our marches generally lasted two or three days. We slept on the trail until we reached an area that my father had previously selected as our hideout. We would camp there for a few weeks until Dad thought it necessary for us to move again.

Usually, we marched during the day but there were times of crisis when we had to escape at night. We walked in the streams whenever possible so as not to leave tracks that the enemy could follow. My brother's worst memory is of the night he dropped the red candy can that Major Villamor had given us in January. The can was Jorge J.'s treasure; he wouldn't let anyone else carry it. As he waded through the mountain stream we were in that night, he stepped into a hole and as he struggled to get his footing, he let go of the red can. It disappeared into the downstream current. My brother tells of the consternation it caused us all. Nothing could be more dangerous than for a Japanese patrol to find that red can. It still had a few lemon drops carefully saved inside, and a couple of "I Shall Return" match books.

My brother remembers that we spent half an hour trying to find, in the dark, the red candy can. My father decided we were losing precious time; we simply had to give up finding the can, trusting God to have it catch beneath the river rocks and rust into nothingness in the years to come.

Jorge Judy Madamba and Helen Madamba as toddlers, circa 1937, Bacolod, Negros Occidental.

Nov. 12, 1940

This photo, dated November 12, 1940, shows a harvested rice field on southern Negros Island. A threshing shed is on the right, with harvest hands stomping rice straw to separate it from the grain. On the left is a dwelling where the farmer's family and workers lived during harvest season. The Madamba family took shelter in structures such as these during their years of concealment, 1942 to 1945.

Staff officers, company commanders, and their junior officers, March 17–31, 1941. Jorge Madamba is third from the right on the first row.

Summer, 1941, in Cartagena, Negros Occidental. Iva and Jorge Madamba pose with their five-year-old son, Jorge J., and eight-year-old daughter, Helen.

Jorge A. Madamba, captain, United States Armed Forces in the Far East (USAFFE), 1945.

An undated photograph, early 1940s. Captain Jorge Madamba, center left, front row, commanded this unit of guerilla soldiers. My father received a battlefield promotion to captain when the guerilla movement was organized. He always wore army khakis and his captain's bars, even though it put him in greater danger were he to be captured. He was determined to maintain military dignity because he knew it was important for troop morale. Note that many of the foot soldiers were without uniforms.

An undated photograph, circa 1945. A victory parade down the main street of a barrio in Negros Occidental.

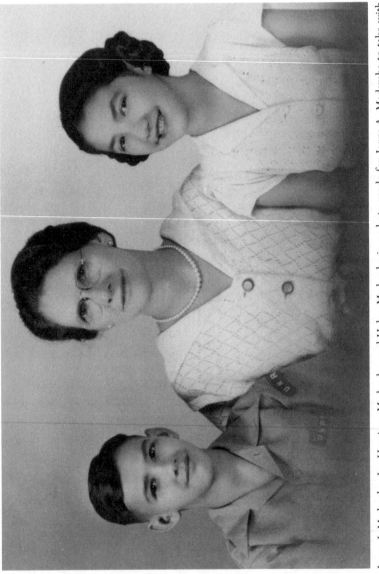

Jorge J. Madamba, Iva Harrison Madamba, and Helen Madamba in a photo made for Jorge A. Madamba to take with him in 1947 on his first United Nations Relief and Rehabilitation Administration assignment in Hunan, China.

The Christmas of '43

The war was in its second year.

I was a little too old for presents because I was old enough to know that there would be none. But I believed, somehow, that Christmas would not go by uncelebrated.

I wasn't disappointed. On Christmas morning, December 25, 1943, there indeed was a present for me to open. It was not just for me but for my brother too and we shared its unveiling. The gift was a ball, 6 or 8 inches in diameter, perhaps the size of a small soccer ball.

Our father and mother smiled at each other as my brother and I played with the ball. They had given us the most perfect gift they could provide, the best Christmas present they had to offer.

I can remember our mother's pride as she told us how she made the ball. We still had among our meager possessions an old, dead tennis ball. Mama cut away the outer layers of the tennis ball and took out the core of hard rubber. She then wound hemp twine, acquired from one of the guerrilla soldiers, around and around the ball until it was the size of a large cantaloupe. Finally Mom took the only silk stocking she had left in her small store of garments and wrapped the stocking tightly around the twine ball. She sewed the stocking down securely to keep the twine from unraveling.

It was a wonder that the ball bounced—but bounce it did. My little brother and I had a great day, tossing and kicking and chasing that ball around as far as we could go. Our play area was limited by forest and boulders, ravines and streams. We could not laugh aloud, we sang Christmas carols in a whisper. When we fell and scraped our knees, we could not cry out in pain; we shed silent tears.

In the jungle, sounds carry distinctly, particularly the sounds of human voices. For many months during the four years of the war, we all had to speak in whispers. Imagine an eight-year-old and a five-year-old confined to whispers—to save their lives.

What our parents had on their minds that day, as Jorge J. and I tossed our Christmas ball, was our survival. They were responsible for keeping us safe from bayonet and bullet, from malnutrition and ultimately starvation, from cholera, amoebic dysentery, malaria, and most of all, from terror—the terror of captivity by Japanese soldiers or Filipino collaborators, from the despair of the concentration camp, the loss of freedom.

Nonetheless, I remember the Christmas of 1943 with joy . . . because of a ball made of the core of a tennis ball, recycled from a previous existence and wrapped in sturdy twine, covered with the last of my mother's silk stockings.

"The Christmas of '43" was first published on December 24, 1989, as my "Hometown" column in the *Woodward News*.

14

My Brother

/ / /

As Japanese troops backed into the hinterlands of the Philippines in 1944, they were forced to make wider forays over Negros Island. There was booty to be had there—rice in storage sheds, fish caught by the villagers and preserved by drying, live chickens and fresh eggs, pigs and dried tapa—and helpless women. The Japanese themselves were cut off from their supply lines. They had to forage for food and military supplies where they could find them. Furthermore, they displaced their own fears by terrorizing the simple country folk who had no way of defending their homes and families.

When my father started the salvage project on the SS *Panay*, he moved us farther into the hills, just below the jungle. It was there that Major Villamor and his special mission established their first radio communication back to General MacArthur in Australia. After Villamor made contact with all of the guerrilla units on Negros, and on the other Visayan islands, he was ordered to move on. Uppermost in his mind was the inevitability that the

Japanese would trace his radio transmissions to our whereabouts. He would not risk our security by remaining in the relative comfort of our hideout.

Soon thereafter, the Japanese established a garrison in Cartagena, our village on the beach, probably because, true to Major Villamor's fears, they knew they were within marching distance of capturing the Madambas. Enemy officers quartered themselves in our plantation house because it was far more pleasant than a nipa hut or an army tent. Whatever the reason for their decision to station a troop deployment in our remote section of the island, it meant immediate danger for my father and our family. The posters offering rewards for information leading to our capture were spread all over the southern region. We moved farther into the jungle to a camp we named Forest Glade. (I take the blame for choosing our place names.)

In the four war years, we were to move nearly a dozen times, not counting the overnight stops where we were simply on our way to somewhere else. We had to keep moving, for to stay in one place for any length of time meant more people would know our location. I have lost track of all the camps where we spent a few days or no more than a couple of weeks or so. Although my father had faith in the loyalty of his fellow soldiers and his friends, he would not take the chance on a fisherman's or farmer's need for the money that was offered for my mother's head, or on the capitulation of a captured guerrillero under torture.

We heard stories of murder and rape and dismemberment, of gouged-out eyes and children mutilated as their parents were forced to watch. My father and mother did their best to keep us from hearing those stories but nonetheless we heard them.

Oddly, the stories did not frighten me that much. I was horrified for those who suffered at the hands of the Japanese but somehow I never saw myself as a victim. I was transported by my reading, my Alice in Wonderland/ Tom Sawyer life of fantasy. I might have been living on a different plane, somewhere else but in the wartime Philippines. The jungle was my Sherwood

Forest, the time in my existence was Arthurian, my language Victorian, and the personae as bodiless as the characters of a costume ball taking place in a midnight dream.

I even created my own Avalon—or maybe it was Shalott—an island where manicured gardens swept down to the edge of the sea. I made a map of that island and marked the locations of castles and mansions where I would one day live. Every night before I went to sleep, I played out a scene of my life on that island. It was always serene.

I don't know if my mother worried about my lack of connection to reality. She too retreated into a reverie of reliving her growing up in western Oklahoma.

Only my brother seemed to have a grip on the here and now. He fished for shrimp and eels and attempted to trap wild chickens to provide us with food. Jorge J. has a wonderful story about his effort to trap a wild chicken for dinner, and how he set the snare and sat silent and motionless behind a self-made blind all day waiting for a wild chicken to go for his bait. He finally caught one very little chicken but he gave up on making chicken a regular part of our menu. In the early 1950s when Jorge J. was a Boy Scout, he attended Philmont Scout Ranch in northern New Mexico, where a Native American demonstrated how to snare a wild chicken.

"It was exactly like the snare I learned to make in the Philippines," my brother said.

During the years we were in the jungle, Jorge J. received a lifetime's education from the guerrilleros, learning about the land and the foliage, the land animals and birds and fish and the weather in the mountain jungle, and mostly the streams and rivers. He absorbed all there was a seven-year-old boy could know about jungle and mountain survival. While I was reading poetry and living in a never-never land of literary fiction, Jorge J. was actively participating in our struggle to survive—and most likely, enjoying it. His memories of our life in the jungle during World War II are different from mine. I cannot presume to tell his story. His own recollections are his to tell. I can only say that his early experience formed the foundation for his success as an athlete in grade school, high school, and college, and colored his joy in raising his son and daughter to be champion competitive swimmers, kayakers, bike-riders, rope climbers, skiers, and lovers of all things out-of-doors. And to this day, my brother in his seventies can best the average thirty-year-old man in most athletic endeavors.

The end of 1943 and the first half of 1944 tested the day-to-day endurance of the Madamba family on Negros Island. For our parents, each dawn was a milestone. We had made it through another night and we would have to face the challenge of staying alive through another day. It was an elemental existence, like being in the intensive care ward of a hospital. We were not conscious of anything except the passage of another hour, another afternoon that ticked by to the beat of a narrow minuet with mortality.

15
Edge of Capture

/ / /

"*Miseez! Miseez! Hapon! Hapon! Run, Miseez, Hapon ees coming!*"

Those dreaded words were gasped in a hoarse whisper by Doroteo as he broke through the jungle underbrush, out of breath, scratched and bleeding, his face ashen.

"Where are they? How far?" Mother asked softly, without a trace of hysteria in her voice.

"Bery near, Miseez! Dere at de guard hut!"

The sentry hut was less than a quarter mile away in a small clearing that overlooked the next ridge between the jungle and the sea.

"Where is Crispin?" Mother asked, referring to another guerrillero on duty with Doroteo.

"Caught, Miseez! Crispin, he caught." Doroteo's face crumpled into tears. "Please, Miseez, run, run. Take de kids and hide. I go dis way—you go de oder way. I make noise. Maybe dey follow me."

We could hear the *whoooooeeeeng* of rifle fire. (I shall never forget that sound.) My mother grabbed my brother and me by the arms, shoving our emergency kits into our hands. She picked up her own bundles of necessities, herded us away from our hut and guided us toward the densest part of the jungle, crouching low almost to a crawl beneath the foliage—and taking advantage of the cover. She seemed to know where we were going. I had never been that far into the wilderness beyond our hut. We crawled and slid our way for about a hundred yards till we reached a high canyon wall. Mother motioned for us to get down on our stomachs and she pushed us through a narrow recess in the rocks.

We were in a small cave, with a ceiling so low Mother had to stoop inside it. It was dark but, when our eyes adjusted to the gloom, we could see each other. Although someone outside looking into the cave would not have been able to distinguish what was inside, we tucked ourselves into the crevices of the rocky cave wall for even more concealment. Amazingly, the cave was pleasantly cool and its floor was fine, soft sand.

"It's a wild pig den," Mother whispered. "When I discovered it, I checked to make sure there weren't any baby pigs in here."

Had I been older, I'm sure my blood would have run cold. I've said earlier that wild pigs were the only animals that we feared in the jungle. And although the cave wasn't currently being occupied, there was a possibility, I think now, that an expectant sow would come in to make the nest ready for a family. It was a measure of my mother's risk-taking personality that she was more willing to face an angry mother hog than to let herself and her children be subjected to captivity or murder by the Japanese.

We huddled in the cave until there was no longer any daylight showing through the narrow crawlspace to the outside. I can't remember being hungry or thirsty or wanting to sleep. If we talked, it was in even quieter whispers than we regularly used outside. Someone asked me not long ago what I thought about while we were hiding and I replied, "I don't think I thought at all."

In the days before we needed a last-resort hiding place, our mother had explored the rocks and cliffs of the jungle around us. She discovered the wild pig den on her own, and decided that was where she would take us if ever there was no place else to run. It was the best she could do. If the Japanese soldiers came up the little trail to our camp, perhaps they would overlook the cave in which we sought shelter. It was one of many such crannies in the jungle; they couldn't search them all.

Mother carried a .38-caliber Colt revolver during those months. Our father had given it to her and I imagine he taught her how to fire it, although I never knew her to do any target practice. I doubt that she had more than six rounds of ammunition and later I had the weird feeling that the bullets were not so much for the Japanese soldiers as they were for the three of us if we were ever taken in captivity. She slept with the gun on the mat next to her head during the most fearful times, but she never used it. I hope now that, when the hostilities were over and we were safe, she threw the gun as far as she could into the Sulu Sea.

Long after darkness, we huddled in the wild pig cave, hearing nothing from outside but the typical sounds of the jungle. Finally, my mother crawled out to assess our circumstances, and minutes later, she returned with my father.

They had devised, months before, a signal between them to be used when they were separated in the jungle. My father alerted us on his returns home by whacking a bolo on a tree trunk three times some distance from our camp. My mother would respond with two bolo whacks to let him know all was well. On this night, Dad came within earshot of our location and gave the signal. After my mother returned the code, they met at the burned-out remains of our little shelter. Mother told him of the Japanese patrol and our harrowing escape from capture.

There was a providential change in my father's route that day. Usually, he took the same faint, narrow trail the Japanese had found that led to our camp. For a reason I never was to know, he and his men walked in over the top of the ridge, not up from the valley. Had he taken the usual path, he would have met the Japanese search party on its way back down to the beach.

My mother related our close call in crawling to the cave. She described how the two guerrilleros saved us from being captured. Dorotheo, a boy of fifteen or sixteen, warned us to hide. The other guard, Crispin, a man in his twenties, had a wife and small children who lived down below near the beach. Crispin typically stayed with us a few days at a time but went home frequently, taking food that we shared with his family, which he earned in lieu of military wages. On that October afternoon, Crispin and Doroteo were pounding rice about a quarter of a kilometer below our hut. They were standing sentry and at the same time hulling rice for our meals, a process too dangerously noisy to be done at the camp. They worked along in the morning quiet, punctuated by the rhythm of the wooden pestles. Occasionally, one of them would stop and mop his forehead with the tail-end of a ragged shirt.

The Japanese patrol came out of the trees below the clearing. Crispin and Doroteo looked up as they heard the sound of rifles being unshouldered. Perhaps they hesitated momentarily, hoping they could answer a few questions and distract the patrol, when suddenly bullets began zinging over their heads. Both men realized that the Japanese soldiers weren't there to exchange pleasantries. Doroteo dived into the tall cogon grass and threw himself down in a gully. He made it to the big trees and overhanging cliffs of the mountain. Hand over hand, he grappled his way through the vines and moss-slick rocks, barely breathing in mortal fear. On his knees, then down on his belly, scrambling through a streambed, grabbing a root for a handhold, dodging branches when he could, then blindly groping through almost solid undergrowth, Doroteo feinted and zagged his way upward through the jungle.

I remember seeing him break through the trees, wild-eyed, bloody with scratches, gasping, "Hapon, Miseez, Hapon! Run, Miseez, run! Hapon ees coming!"

Crispin was captured and we had to get away. Mother knew Crispin could not bear interrogation torture for very long. It was just a matter of time until he would bring the Japanese to our camp.

Later, we were told Crispin did endure long enough for us to flee. After hours of unspeakable pain from terrible beatings, hunger, and dehydration, he finally took the Japanese to our burned-out shelter and confirmed that we had lived there. Our escape trail was cold by then and the Japanese knew they would have to wait until another day to bring in the Madamba family. Crispin was released and he made it back to his home, to his wife and children, and his aged parents, where he collapsed on his doorstep and soon died.

16

Flight through Fear

/ / /

We began our march toward another hideout at the first light of dawn after we slept a few hours in the wild pig den. The first night of the march we stopped to eat and sleep, and my father went on without us to arrange for another hideout. It was still daylight and Mother started lighting the cooking fire. The few matches she had would light but wouldn't stay lit long enough to catch damp kindling on fire. As she struck each one without success, a little pile of dead matchsticks grew. Mother was not given to panic but I could tell she was worried that her family might not eat that night. One of the guerrilleros offered to go looking for a particular shrub or tree with oily leaves, so he took off and we waited, hungry, for him to return. In a while he came back with an armload of leafy branches and Mother tried again. Still the matches would not burn the leaves, and she turned on the poor man and berated him.

"You said you know what to get for the fire," she said. "These aren't the right leaves and none of us will have rice or viands tonight." It was the only time I ever heard her raise her voice in anger against a guerrillero.

With vicious determination, she struck another match and miraculously a little flame started up under the cooking pot. One more time during those desperate hours, a greater power took care of us.

We walked through the jungle for three more days. When it rained we took shelter in hollow tree trunks or small caves beneath the outcroppings of cliffs, or beneath broad-leafed elephant-ear plants. The rain was not cold and it provided respite from the jungle heat.

One late afternoon we found shelter in an abandoned threshing shed in the middle of a kaingin clearing. By now my mother was visibly exhausted and wanted to spend another day there just to rest, but my father, who had just returned from his search for a haven for us, made us get up and get going before daylight because we could too easily be picked off by rifle fire in that vulnerable open field.

Except for that one night, we camped by mountain streams. There we were protected by jungle cover, and my little brother could set his shrimp traps.

When we finally reached an open hillside on the fourth day, my mother collapsed. She said she could not go on.

"Where are we running to?" she asked.

"To a safer place," my father said.

"And where is that safer place?" my mother said. "There is no safer place. You don't have any idea where we're going. I cannot walk any farther and neither can the children. We can only stay here or die."

"We will die if we stay here," said my father. "We are still too close to the beach. There are barrios down there, barrios where the Japs are in control. When they find out that we are less than a day's march away, they will come and get us. We cannot protect ourselves in an open firefight. We don't have the ammunition and we don't have the men.

"Then let them," my mother said. "Let them find us and I will give myself up."

"Are you saying you will surrender?" my father said in disbelief. "No, you will not surrender. I will never surrender. Never. And you will not die, not here, not with our children, and not with me. You cannot surrender because what will happen to you will be worse than dying. You are an American woman and you have two small children that you must live for. You are the last American free in these mountains and there is a price on your head as there is a price on my head. What they will do to us, if we are caught, is more horrible than you can imagine."

My father raged on. I can only paraphrase his declaration. "I am not going to give up for an even more important reason. If you give up, and I give up then there is nothing left—for these boys who are with us, risking their lives for our safety, for the Philippines, for America, and most of all for our children. We may all die while we are running, while we are hiding, but we will not die like pigs in a slaughterhouse. We will not die begging for mercy. We will not die defeated. No, I will not surrender until the United States surrenders—and neither will you."

I had never heard my soft-spoken gentle father speak in those tones before, and certainly not to my mother. Mother was the assertive one, the decision maker, the rule enforcer, and the unequivocal leader who always knew what to do next.

At that moment I hated my dad. How could he speak so harshly to my mother? She was the one who virtually carried us up the mountains, who found us a hiding place when the Japanese soldiers had us within firing range, and she was the one who always, always told us we would someday live in Oklahoma and go to college at Oklahoma A&M. I was frightened because Mother was so sick. How would we survive if she could not take care of us?

I watched her crouched on a fallen tree trunk, ants crawling up her bare white legs, her head in her arms, her auburn red hair sticking to her neck with sweat, her shoulders shaking with her sobs.

My mother's next act of desperation terrified me even more. She was burning with fever and there was no water nearby for her to drink. We had four Orange Crush sodas in our emergency packs. We were carrying them to open in celebration when the war ended. Mother grabbed one of the Orange Crush bottles and broke off its neck on a rock. She tipped the jagged bottle up to her lips and gulped down the soda. The liquid ran down over her face and she drank all that went into her mouth. She didn't care if shards of glass cut her throat.

Dear Dad: Now I know what you had to do. You could not let your wife Iva, your strong helpmate and beacon of life, give up. You knew how sick she was with malaria, and you were also sick, with a pain in your groin that forced you to limp as you climbed through the jungle. Physically, neither of you could endure much more. But you refused to go down because of your children. You would not let us be left defenseless.

And so we struggled on. We crawled over the rocks and cliffs, we waded down the mountain streams and under ancient gigantic trees of nara, mahogany, and luaun. Each night Mother cooked us a meal in the middle of the jungle. My little brother diligently brought in the shrimp and eels he had trapped. The guerrilleros soldiered on beside us, carrying heavy sacks of rice and the rest of our household supplies, and keeping their pitifully decrepit rifles at the ready. Were we to encounter the Japanese army, none of us would survive.

17

The Killing Waters

/ / /

We walked for another day to reach the spot that Dad had chosen for our next
encampment. It was on a small, beautiful mountain meadow. We could
look out across the lowlands to the Sulu Sea. It was a breathtaking location.
We stood on the highest ridge of southern Negros with the jungle all around
below us and we could see over the trees and the surrounding countryside.

"We can stay here," said my father. "I think it is safe here."

For Mother, it was a release from jungle claustrophobia. We called that
camp "Blue Sky."

In the summer of 1944, the pall began to lift and our spirits began to
rise. The guerrilla army in the Philippines became an even more important
component in the war to liberate the islands. American bombers blasted
the industrial areas of northern Negros. The military installations and supply
depots of the Japanese were under heavy air attack and along with them
the sugar mills and refineries, the beautiful Spanish colonial and Chinese

mansions that were confiscated to house Japanese officers, the highways and bridges, telephone and power lines, electrical plants and school buildings, granaries and churches and civic centers—any building that the Japanese had taken over to house its war machine. The guerrilleros were responsible for gathering information about the targets and reporting by radio to U.S. air forces where to concentrate their bombs.

Filipino troops were charged with the task of rescuing American pilots who had been shot down at sea. I don't know how many of those flyers my father and his men saved, but there were enough that the guerrillas knew their effort had a role in the winning of the war. My father's soldiers watched for the sight of white parachutes floating down. Then they raced out into the surf, paddling their sleek little bancas to retrieve U.S. airmen bobbing up and down in the waves. The guerrilleros pulled them aboard, paddled them back to land, kept them safe in someone's nipa home, tended their wounds, and signaled for a rescue seaplane.

Japanese pilots also went down in our waters. My father observed one of the falling enemy planes and saw two parachuting survivors. The guerrillas were not so eager to perform a rescue but they saw the two pilots make it to a tiny coral atoll within swimming distance of the mainland. By this time, Japanese troops stationed in Cartagena had been pulled out and sent back north.

Through binoculars supplied by a MacArthur submarine, the guerrilleros scanned the atoll during the day and posted guards at night to make sure the Japanese airmen didn't escape. For seven days, the soldiers watched the survivors on the atoll. There was no evidence that they had water except for whatever they could catch in their helmets during afternoon rainstorms, and they may have been able to catch a fish or two to eat. By the end of the seventh day, my father decided it was time for the guerrilleros to take the pilots prisoner. He ordered out two bancas, boarded the lead boat, and headed to the atoll. As the bancas approached the tiny coral island, my father called out to the Japanese pilots to surrender. Japanese was one language my father did not speak. He called to them in Vasayan, Tagalog, and English.

The airmen huddled in crevices of the rock. Cautiously, my father and his men pulled up to the atoll and climbed ashore, under cover of rifles leveled from the second boat. Once again, Dad called upon the Japanese flyers to surrender and got no response. Finally, the guerrilleros moved forward, grabbed the enemy airmen, and forced them into the bancas, one in each boat.

The pilots were weak, clearly debilitated from their seven-day ordeal on the rock. They were unarmed and truly at the mercy of their captors. My father held out a canteen of water to the prisoner in his boat and the man took advantage of that gesture of kindness to break free and jump into the sea.

"Dumolog! Dumolog!" the Filipinos shouted. Stop! Stop!

The pilot continued to swim away. Warning shots were fired beyond him and still he swam, widening the distance between himself and the bancas. Finally, a guerrillero sharpshooter in the rear boat aimed directly at the fleeing airman and shot him dead.

Once again, there was a conversation I was not supposed to hear when my father came home. He and Mother always talked in the early hours of morning, perhaps when they were most at peace and when they thought my brother and I were asleep.

I listened to my dad tell my mother in a hollow, breaking voice. "That poor man. The sea turned red with his blood. He rolled over in the water and looked at me—and we were looking directly at each other, face to face, when he died."

With the war clearly coming to a close and the Philippines about to be liberated, my father was in a frenetic hurry to be everywhere. The communications network he organized became an efficient system of coast watchers. Intelligence teams infiltrated the towns and villages near Japanese military bases and fed information back to U.S. headquarters concerning troop emplacements, battle plans, and strategic installations. Soldiers who were sixteen-year-old boys when they first joined my father's army now had three and a half years experience in covert fighting and were seasoned for open battle. Old farmers and fishermen who could neither read nor write provided invaluable intelligence about wind currents, weather changes, tides, and other signs of nature—the colors of leaves, the complexion of the sea and the jungle and fields. They sensed distant sounds that meant nothing to anyone else, sounds that proved vital when translated to military planners.

The guerrilleros were finally on the march, confident, capable, in control, invincible in their determination to be rid of the Japanese. The fishing villages below us became fishing villages again, not garrisons of enemy troops. The occupation army pulled out quickly, recalled by their commanders to make a last fatal stand on some more important battlefield.

June 14, 1944, began disastrously for me. I had an earache. The left side of my head pulsated with excruciating pain. Beginning in the hours of early morning, my mother cradled me in her arms, rocking me to the rhythm of her whispering voice. There was nothing to alleviate my pounding agony, no aspirin, no decongestant, no sedative, no antihistamine or antibiotic, not even a hot water bottle. My mother held warm wet clothes over my ear, trying to calm me and keep me from wailing because we still didn't dare make loud human sounds.

By midday I had gone through a series of fevers and cold baths of perspiration, of wracking, throbbing, convulsive spasms of pain in my infected ear. Mother held me through all those hours, laying me on a sleeping mat for only a few minutes when the pain lessened so she could keep the fire going under the water kettle.

About midafternoon, as she sat on the ground rocking me in her arms, I heard her whisper, "Oh, my goodness!" I looked up and saw what she saw. Across the horizon of the ocean was a very shadowy dark outline of a ship. As we watched it move north, another ship came behind it and then another and another. Soon the entire long edge of the seascape was filled with ships of all sizes—flat ones, tall ones, ships as tiny as flyspecks, and others that were certainly, at that distance, immense. The perimeter of the ocean was filled with vessels so close together it was as if the skyline were joined to the near shore in one endless naval armada. And above them were airplanes, some circling, some fanning out to the east and west, sweeping the edges of the sky like seagulls hunting for prey. We gazed, hypnotized at the sight.

"Do you think they're the Americans, Mama?" I said.

"I don't know," she said. "Whatever they are, something very big is going to happen."

For sixty years I've wondered what we saw on the Sulu Sea that day in 1944, Flag Day as our mother had reminded us first thing that morning. Recently, in reading historians' accounts of the sea battles in the Pacific, I learned that the First Mobile Fleet of the Imperial Japanese Navy passed through Guimaras Strait between Negros and Panay islands on June 14, 1944. The armada stopped to refuel in the strait, then sailed on toward the Marianas where it met the United States Navy in the Battle of the Philippine Sea. It was the defeat of the Japanese Navy that spelled the coming of the end of World War II.

I sensed, just as my mother and my brother did, and the guerrillero sentries who so faithfully cared for us and commiserated with us and shared our danger did, that victory was in sight. Those ships gathered in the Guimaras Strait of the Sulu Sea were the last of one of the greatest navies of history, on their way to Armageddon in the Philippines Sea.

U.S. sailors would refer to the battle as the Marianas Turkey Shoot because the vaunted Japanese Navy was all but destroyed within two days. U.S. ground troops, however, were not so lucky. The fighting on Saipan, Tinian, Guam, and Iwo Jima are recorded historically as fields of carnage and, although American Marines and infantrymen fought valiantly and won, the cost in lives was heartbreakingly dear.

Despite the decisive naval battles in the Philippines Sea and later in Leyte Gulf, it would be October 1944 before General MacArthur could stride through the surf onto Philippine soil and declare, "I have returned."

18

Blue Sky

/ / /

From June to October, we waited in Blue Sky for our Americans to come. Even though we were certain, at last, that the war was ending and that the Philippines would be liberated, our own situation was still in doubt. My father and mother were fearful that diehard Japanese soldiers or Filipino collaborators seeking reprisal might still be looking for us.

We were not willing to risk moving down out of the jungle, but my parents did what they could to normalize our life style. We no longer had to whisper when we talked. The mountain meadow on which our last nipa hideout was built was broad enough to allow for Mother's garden. We even had a couple of horses brought up from the valley, and my brother and I took turns riding. Mother had grown up on the back of a horse in northwest Oklahoma and Dad brought her a white pony named Victor. Although the little Arabian was much smaller than the farm mares of her childhood, she reveled in having a horse of her own again. During our wearisome treks into the mountains, Mother occasionally groaned, "Oh, I'd give anything for one of my daddy's mules."

While we remained up in the hills, it was obvious my brother and I were desperately in need of clothing. We had outgrown the shirts and shorts, skirts and pants that we had when the war started. We wore them anyway because size didn't matter, but they were not much more than rags. Both Jorge J. and I were small for our age, probably because of our wartime (or Asian) diet, but we caught up after coming to the United States.* Our feet continued to grow normally during those four years, however, and we had no shoes. We literally went barefoot until we arrived in America.

Mother was anticipating the end of the war and she wanted us properly dressed when it arrived. At my urging she decided to try out a kind of cloth of pounded bark that kaingin women used for clothing. Even as a child I was evidently a fashionista, eager to wear the most outrageous outfits I saw. Mom obtained a yard or so of the "fabric" and proceeded to make me a dress. It was not a successful experiment. The dress fit well enough, but it smelled like tree sap. Worst of all, it was scratchy and stiff and the skirt stood out from my body like screen wire. We decided the dress wasn't worth saving so we threw it out. It was one of the few times Mother wasted anything, especially something on which she had spent her time.

We marked the days at Blue Sky, settling into a routine of waiting.

After American forces landed on Leyte in October, my father brought us home to the lowlands. We rode down from the mountains on horse-back, with our treasured books and cooking utensils, our meager items of clothing, and what was left of our food supply, all of it pulled on a carabao sled, the luxury of which we did not have while we were fleeing through the jungle.

---

*Today, my brother is six feet three and I'm five feet six. Our Harrison genes kicked in after the war.

Dad had built a nice home for us in a place I named Victory House. It wasn't on the beach—he still had reservations about our possible exposure to the retreating Japanese—but it was a real house that was open and airy and we could run and play and shout and sing and laugh and cry without fear. Every day or so, American airplanes flew overhead and we could see U.S. Army and U.S. Navy insignia on their wings and we wept with joy. As a precaution, my father placed an American flag on the roof so the pilots wouldn't mistake our larger-than-usual home for a Japanese emplacement. More than once, I saw a fighter dip his wings in greeting. We waved our arms and screamed our hearts out in thankfulness and welcome.

19

The Life March

/ / /

American troops did not land on Negros until early 1945. The fighting for the liberation of our island has been given short shrift in at least one historical account that I've read recently, but a veteran of that jungle campaign calls it the most vicious of the entire war—and he had been through New Guinea and the south Pacific as a paratrooper-foot soldier.

Perhaps it was the battle, or battles, for Negros that most completely molded my feelings about the Pacific War after I was thirty years old. Somehow, I came to realize that what my family had endured from 1942 to 1945 was not a walk in the park, not an exercise in political grandeur. Although some historians have given an impression that Negros was an afterthought, I know it was not. My friend the paratrooper who fought to liberate Negros Island deserves not to be called extraneous, even as the men and women who died in the Malinta Tunnel on Corregidor after MacArthur left don't deserve to be considered expendable.

As soon as it was possible for my father to hand over the leadership of his quartermaster corps to a subordinate officer, and get orders cut (he might even have cut the orders himself) for him to report to U.S. military headquarters in Bacolod, the province's capital city, he traveled north. He vowed to my mother that he would move heaven and earth to make it possible for us to go to the United States, war or no war. World War II was not yet over and wouldn't be for six more months.

As soon as my father was fairly confident that American citizens were to be repatriated to the United States, he sent a guerrillero courier to us in southern Negros to fetch us to Bacolod. Once again we were on the march, but it was no longer a march of escape. We were going to Bacolod, we were going to be repatriated. Although we didn't know the words, we were going to San Francisco.

Mother, Jorge J., and I set out from Victory Hill, a home we had come to love during the few months that we lived there, knowing we would never see it again. With the courier leading the way, we walked the seaside trail from Cartagena to Cauayan, to the highway. It took us two days to make the thirty-kilometer trek. We spent the night in a friend's nipa shack along the way. After we reached the highway, we still had fifty or so kilometers to go before we reached the city of Bacolod. The highway was pockmarked with bomb craters and we had to walk around them, adding distance to our destination. The old asphalt of the road was broken and rough on our bare feet. Jorge J. and Mother and I could barely endure the pain. We had walked barefoot through the mountains for three years, but our feet were accustomed to the texture of natural terrain, not to the searing black surface of desiccated pavement.

Soon after we reached the highway, we saw our first American soldiers, our liberators. They were coming toward us in an army Jeep, five GIs, bearing down on us with incredible speed—perhaps thirty miles per hour. We had been joined by other walking refugees, so there was quite a crowd of us trudging along.

The Jeep came roaring through as all of us jumped to the side of the highway, whooping and hollering with joy, screaming and waving our arms in welcome. The five American soldiers in the Jeep looked at us incredulously, probably amazed that anyone could be walking on that broken road on such a torrid day. We didn't care how foolish we appeared. For me, it was worth the sight of their sun-browned faces, their gray-green clothing, and their innocent, questioning eyes.

I hoped that some of them saw my mother, my mother with the auburn-red hair and the freckled nose and the sunburned hands, and knew that she was an American, their sister, their cousin, their high school classmate, or their aunt. She wasn't old enough to be a soldier's mother, perhaps, but didn't she represent those beautiful, hardworking women that they had all left at home?

My cousin Bill Harrison from Ellis County, Oklahoma, was in Negros at that same time. He was a nineteen-year-old freshman at Oklahoma A&M when he enlisted in the army and was assigned to the Signal Corps. While his older brother Jack was crawling under fire through the coral detritus on Iwo Jima, Bill was flying into Leyte when he was wounded in a battle he never described to his family—at least not to me. Relegated to a casualty camp in Tacloban, Bill decided after a few days that he wasn't injured enough to stay confined in a hospital tent. He somehow checked himself out and managed to hitch an airplane ride to Negros, where he went to look for his "Aunt Johnny," his family's pet name for my mother. Bill's father, my uncle Marshall, the only son in a family that had six girls, longed for a brother, and when my mother was due to be born, Marshall had a name ready. It didn't matter that the youngest sibling was yet again another girl. She was "Johnny" to Marshall for the rest of their lives. Bill Harrison perhaps passed us like the proverbial ship in the night. By the time he arrived in Negros to search for his Aunt Johnny, we probably were in the casualty camp in Leyte that he had just left.

After the Jeep with the American servicemen went by, we continued our dogged slogging north. We spent the next night of our journey in the sugar-mill town of Binalbagan, where Aunt Charlotte had lived. Again, we stayed with a family with which my father had made previous arrangements. That evening, the guerrillero with us decided to take a sightseeing walk for a closeup view of the wreckage of the refinery that had been destroyed by American bombers. I tagged along and I remember, as we walked through the ruined buildings, the distinct odor of decomposing corpses.

It was still a long way to our destination, to U.S. Army headquarters in Bacolod. After another day on the road, we were beginning to play out. My brother and I were very weary and no amount of roadside rest breaks made it easier for us. We were passed, time and again, by ancient trucks and decrepit cars, chugging along not much faster than we were walking, carefully skirting the bomb craters and other obstacles in the highway, loaded to the gills with passengers and freight. Mother attempted to flag them down for a ride but they ignored her and drove on. Weighted down as they were, it was no wonder they would not take on hitchhikers.

Late in the fourth or perhaps the fifth day on our road, my mother had had enough. Jorge J. and I were seriously lagging. For me, putting one bare foot in front of the other was agonizing.

What had once been a public transit bus hove into view going our direction. Even from a distance we could see it was swamped with riders. There were arms and legs protruding from all openings, suitcases and baskets and bundles stacked four deep on its top, and chicken coops hanging from its sides. My mother had made up her mind. Putting on her steel armor of determination, she strode out into the middle of the highway, waving her arms. She was not going to move and the bus finally squealed to a stop a few feet short of running her down, and we, including our guerrillero escort, clambered on. The riders already on the bus graciously scooted even closer to each other to make room for us. What friends we had, even in those few minutes!

When we arrived in Bacolod, my father was there to greet us with thankful tears. And who else could be there beside him but our wonderful Aunt Charlotte, whom we thought had been executed in 1943! She was alive and as haughty and self-assured as ever. The reports of her death by hanging at the hands of the Japanese had been grossly exaggerated, probably by those who thought she had hanging coming.

True to character, Aunt Charlotte had already made connections with the American liberators. The handsome young officers of the U.S. Army were frequent guests in her home, probably drawn by her two beauteous teenage daughters who sometime during the war had managed to come home from Manila. Aunt Charlotte knew who to see about repatriation to the States. She made friends with one especially influential young man, a major from San Francisco, whom she called Bob. When I lived in Northern California years later, I read newspaper stories about the man, by then a high-profile industrialist and civic leader in the Bay Area.

For several weeks my parents were investigated and interrogated and asked to sign papers and we waited for the channels of military bureaucracy to clear our way to go to America. In another of the mystical convergences of World War II, the officer assigned to check us out happened to be a young man from Woodward, Oklahoma. He was Turner Quisenberry, the son of the pastor of my mother's hometown church. He worked in the Civilian Investigation Commission, the CIC, a forerunner of the CIA. It didn't take him long to substantiate my mother's claim that she was an American citizen, and that she had not engaged in activities to help the enemy.

An evening shortly thereafter, we were told to prepare to leave for Leyte in the morning, all of us except my father and Aunt Charlotte. The U.S. government hadn't quite made up its mind how to classify my father. He was not an American citizen, yet he was an American military officer. He was the spouse of an American, but in 1945 that did not entitle him to free passage and entry to the United States—especially since he was a male spouse and therefore theoretically not a dependent. There was even a problem with my status. Because I was born before 1936, I was, in the eyes of the government, legally of my father's nationality, a Filipina, an alien. Three years later the Congress of the United States declared all children of Americans U.S. citizens, no matter where they were born and even if they had a foreign father.

Someone with compassion who was in a decision-making position declared that because of my tender years, I would be allowed to go with my mother to America. My father convinced my mother not to quibble, and although our family had never been separated during World War II, she finally acceded to leaving him and going home.

Aunt Charlotte, on the other hand, was indisputably an American. There was no question as to her citizenship. She was, however, the subject of gossip and innuendo, and the spite and enmity of those determined to avenge the slights she had inflicted upon them in years past. Questions were raised anonymously about her loyalty, and slanders were reported because she had managed to stay out of a concentration camp when other Americans were doomed to die there.

"It is the eleventh hour," Aunt Charlotte raged, watching my mother ready us for the first leg of our journey to the United States. "In the eleventh hour, I am prevented from going home."

Crosses

My mother and I sat in a Quonset hut, one of those galvanized metal half-cylinder buildings that the Seabees (construction battalions) put together like giant toys overnight. It was the office of the military administration and command, set up as soon as the U.S. Army gained a foothold on what had been enemy-held territory. A young first lieutenant was explaining to my mother the process by which her family could be repatriated to the United States. He questioned her to determine if she had a legitimate right to a free ride on a troop ship, checked her passport, my father's passport, my brother's birth record and mine, my parents' marriage certificate, and all the other papers Mother so carefully carried with her throughout the war.

The metal folding chairs we sat on were uncomfortably warm in the morning heat. I tried not to squirm, tried to keep my mind on the officer and my mother's conversation, but my eyes wandered past the desk and the papers on it, and I saw, leaning crookedly against the concave metal wall, a wooden cross about three feet high, painted white. On the horizontal bar of the cross was a name, neatly stenciled in black, **Robert Howard, Cpl. USMC**, and yesterday's date.

For a moment I wasn't sure what it meant. I stared at it until I realized why the cross was there. Even then, I felt no reaction except curiosity. The name fascinated me. It was so American, so crisp, so honest-sounding, so innocent, so clean. Somewhere behind a sugar mill or in some cane field or on a jungle ridge or narrow wooden bridge across a muddy river, Robert Howard had been killed in one of the last days of this interminably barbarous war. It must have happened not far from here because, within a few hours after his death, someone during the night stenciled his fine clean name on a white cross to mark his grave.

My mother rose to leave and I trailed after her to the door as she thanked the young officer for his help. We walked out into the sun and I looked beyond the Quonset hut to the landscape behind it, seeing something I had not noticed before. Over the low hills, as far as my eyes could take me, were rows and rows of fresh white crosses, lined up so neatly they made geometric patterns that glimmered in the morning light. I did not look up at my mother, hoping she wouldn't follow my gaze, that she would walk away without seeing what I had seen. We did not speak but in my mind there shone a thousand Robert Howards who would forever lie in this beautiful, broken land, this land that I was leaving. I was going to the country that they had called home. They would remain here, in the country where I was born.

20

Greater Love Hath No Man

/ / /

He was nineteen years old. He had signed up to be a paratrooper after he'd volun- teered at his local selective service office in Linwood, California. When he went into the military service of the United States, it was 1943 and he hadn't finished high school.

He is now in his eighties, handsome, distinguished, a man of faith and clear vision.

"We jumped into Noumia. Then we went by boat to Leyte and then to Corregidor. After that we went to Negros," said Wayne Ruttman, sixty years later.

The crack paratroopers, teenage daredevils who left their homes for glory and out of an incredible sense of duty, became foot soldiers, slogging through ridge and valley of tropical terrain.

From 1943 to 1945, Ralph Wayne Ruttman fought as a soldier in the United States Army in the rain-besotted, green jungle-walls of the South

Pacific, and then the Philippines. There were two other Mooreland, Oklahoma, soldiers in his outfit. They were Billy Fields and Art Dezort. When they were children the three boys went to grammar school in Curtis, held in a one-room schoolhouse just a few miles east of Mooreland. Now, half a century after Wayne Ruttman and Art Dezort and Billy Fields hauled rifles into the Melanesian jungles, the three are living out their lives in Woodward County, revered, respected and remembered. They were gorgeous young nineteen-year-olds in 1943. Now they are even stronger men who have earned the love and esteem of the generations who follow them.

When I think of Tom Brokaw's book, *The Greatest Generation*, I think of Art Dezort.

Art and I belong to St. John's Episcopal Church. We see each other nearly every Sunday morning. He has his own pew—we call it Art's Pew—at the back of the church. Other members of the congregation sit with him from time to time but it's called Art's Pew because that's where he always is.

Art is a war hero. He was all but blown apart on Corregidor as American troops took back the fortified rock that stands guard at the entrance of Manila Harbor. Manila, one of the most densely populated and largest land-area cities of the world, is the capital of the Philippines. It was declared an open city by General MacArthur in the final weeks of 1941, to save it from destruction by Japanese invaders. Corregidor fell to the Japanese in 1942. In 1945 it was liberated by American soldiers like Art Dezort. They were the soldiers of the 503rd Regimental Combat Team.

Dezort enlisted in the army while he was a high school senior in 1943. He knew he was going to be drafted as soon as he graduated, so he joined up and volunteered to go to paratrooper school because it meant $50 more pay a month. Besides, said Dezort, jumping out of an airplane sounded more exciting than just shooting a gun. After training at Fort Benning, Georgia, Art found himself in the South Pacific when he reached his nineteenth birthday on June 2, 1944. In that vast beyond of ocean and tropic foliage and incessant rain, mud, and mosquitoes, he was about as far from northwest Oklahoma as he could get. One day, on one of those South Seas islands, Art ran into another paratrooper, Wayne Ruttman. He too was from Mooreland. Ruttman was living in California when he enlisted, but his family moved back home to Oklahoma shortly thereafter. Wayne and Art remembered each other well as classmates in the one-room school at Curtis, a hamlet just east of Mooreland.

"Wayne was in Headquarters Company of the 1st Battalion," said Dezort. "He had rank—he was a Pfc." Dezort, a buck private, was a member of Company C.

For all their elite training as paratroopers, both Dezort and Ruttman were still infantrymen—and when they were on the ground, they were front-line combat soldiers. After months of island hopping and jungle warfare, the 503rd landed on Leyte, a big island on the eastern side of the Philippine archipelago.

"We were there during that huge naval battle, the Battle of Leyte Gulf," said Ruttman.

"The Japanese navy was shelling the landing area when we went ashore," said Dezort. "We was diggin' fox holes faster'n a backhoe."

The 503rd was then sent from Leyte to Mindoro, an island south and west of Manila, where it was poised to retake Corregidor. In a memoir, Harold Templeman, an unarmed noncombatant civilian Red Cross worker who went in with the troops, wrote:

Big lumbering C-47s of the 317th Troop Carrier Group had passed over the Rock's famed 'topside' to belch forth their cargo of Yank paratroopers. Tumbling out of the big planes' doors, one by one the tiny dark specks blossomed out into billowing parachutes with hard-hitting hunks of men, armed to the teeth, dangling from the suspension lines.

Down and down they crashed onto the bomb-pocked parade ground, through the roofs of wrecked concrete and steel buildings, into tall trees and scrub undergrowth, over the sides of the sheer cliffs and into the rubble and debris left by hundreds of tons of bombs and naval shells. For two hours they dropped before the planes turned back toward Mindoro to bring more and more paratroopers.

Templeton published the slim softcover memoir titled *The Return to Corregidor* in 1945. Ruttman has a cherished copy of the book, and as I asked him questions about the recapture of that fortress island, he said quietly, "It's all in the book."

The First Battalion, Dezort and Ruttman's unit, went in on amphibious landing craft the day after the initial jump. The delay may have saved their lives because the first wave of paratroopers that was air-dropped was decimated in the hazardous terrain and a twenty-mile-an-hour crosswind. It took two weeks to secure the Rock. During that time, American troops were ordered to root out all enemy soldiers barricaded in the island's volcanic caves.

Monkey Point was the spot where the Japanese made their last stand on the island of Corregidor. Dezort, Ruttman, and their superior officer, Second Lieutenant George Conn, were ordered to clear away the fortifications blocking the entrance to the Monkey Point cave. As they worked, a horrendous explosion shook the Rock and threw debris as far as 2,000 yards into the sea. The lieutenant was killed. Ruttman was thrown out of the blast. Dezort was nowhere to be found. Ruttman searched for his fellow townsman for days and could not find him. He finally believed that Dezort was dead.

On the same day that Dezort disappeared in the Monkey Point blast, American warships began steaming into Manila Bay, bringing in more troops and supplies to end the war in the Philippines. Ruttman and what was left of the First Battalion once again boarded the amphibian LSTs, this time bound for the island of Negros.

With American forces closing in and around the Philippines in late 1944, the Japanese decided to fortify Negros. Perhaps they recognized that Negros had the food supply that would sustain them in a long siege. Perhaps they hoped that the virgin jungle would provide them concealment in their last stand. The Japanese knew that none of them were ever going to return to Japan by their own means. If they were all to die, they would do it fighting to the last man in the dense mountain ranges of interior Negros, the same sanctuary that their adversaries, guerrilleros and fugitive Americans, had sought throughout the years since 1942.

Wayne Ruttman said the fight on Negros was the most physically grueling of the entire war.

"We hiked over ridge after ridge, in combat most of the way," he said. "And at the top of every ridge, there was another ridge to climb. The mountain range was endless. And the Japanese were dug into every rock and behind every tree—and up in the top of the trees."

Casualties were enormous. Day after day, the dead and wounded American soldiers were carried down out of the mountains. They were buried in a military cemetery outside the city of Bacolod.

Into this cauldron of weariness and terror, who should show up, reporting for duty with the 503rd but Art Dezort. Ruttman was astounded.

"I thought he was dead," said Ruttman.

Dezort had been critically wounded in the explosion at Monkey Point. He was evacuated to a field hospital, where his most serious injury was to one of his eyes, which had been struck by a fragment of rock. When Dezort returned to Oklahoma at the end of the war, a doctor advised him to have the eye surgically removed because it was impairing the vision in his good eye. He followed the doctor's advice.

As Dezort recovered from his injuries in the field hospital nearest Corregidor, he was in line to be rotated home, but the waiting went on too long and he was tired of being sidelined. He asked to go back to the First Battalion of the 503rd—and so it was that he was once again fighting alongside his fellow townsman, Wayne Ruttman, on the island of Negros.

There is an axiom that has been taken for granted for as long as I can remember. It says the young are conscripted into military service because they are fearless; they think they're immortal.

We have always sent our young into battle. We call them soldier boys because that's what they are—barely older than children. They fought valiantly in World War II because that's what they were expected to do, and they wanted to win that war or die trying.

But Wayne Ruttman put the lie to the axiom.

"The nights were the worst. There were times at night when I thought I would die of fear."

"Greater Love Hath No Man" was first published in the *Woodward News* in November 1998.

21

The Eleventh Hour

/ / /

In early June 1945, Jorge J., Mother and I, along with a lot of wounded and sick soldiers, boarded an LCT—landing craft for troops—an iron barge with straight sides that wallowed in the ocean. Once inside the barge, passengers could not see out. It was like traveling in the bottom of a bathtub or a barrel, subjected to the toss of the waves with nothing as a point of reference. The LCT had a small superstructure that provided the only shelter from the sun.

Within an hour or so after we left the dock on Negros, I began to vomit. Over the previous three months, I had been showing the symptoms of incipient malaria, shaking with chills in the late afternoon, then burning with fever throughout the night, and getting gradually weaker day by day. I was very underweight. Hour after hour on that heaving landing craft, I retched and gagged while sympathetic sailors and soldiers tried to help my mother ease my agony. Finally, the officer in charge invited my mother to take me into the wheelhouse, and one of the GIs gave her a very ripe apple, which she scraped to a pulp with a borrowed pocket knife, feeding it to me in tiny portions off the edge of the blade. It tasted good but I couldn't swallow it because of the contractions of my throat and esophagus. There were no fluids on the landing craft except canteen water, which was heavily laced with chlorine, and probably hardly any food. Most of the soldiers who traveled with us were themselves sick or wounded, but they were more concerned about my suffering than they were about themselves, and none of them had a mother to care for them as I did.

The trip between Negros and Leyte lasted thirty-six hours, I think. My mother later referred to my ailment as "seasickness," a humiliating term for something that almost took my life. Like Aunt Charlotte, I very nearly didn't make it at the eleventh hour.

I was almost comatose when we landed in Leyte. An ambulance transported me to the Tacloban field hospital and I lay on an army cot in a tent for days. It was a women's ward, where there were four or five WACs and army nurses almost as sick as I. I was dosed with massive amounts of Atabrine and canned fruit juices and some sort of soft food. In those days, there was no intravenous fluid procedure, so the best that could be done for dehydration was to coax me to swallow as much liquid as possible. By the third or fourth day, I was able to comprehend where I was.

Sometime during my hospital stay, my father and Aunt Charlotte arrived on Leyte. The American military command had decided my father could accompany his family to the United States so he could be treated in a U.S. veteran's hospital for an inguinal hernia that was approaching the critical stage. Now I imagine it was my father's influence, for a change, that set Aunt Charlotte free. After she landed at Tacloban, Aunt Charlotte spent hours at my cot-side in the field hospital, reading to me, giving me drinks of water and juice, and spooning food into my mouth. I laughed at the way she made a face when she took a tiny taste of my hospital food. What a blessing it was for my mother and dad to have Aunt Charlotte with them to see me through those most perilous days of my life.

The women who were my fellow patients fascinated me. They looked so much like my mother—and I had seen few people in my lifetime who resembled my mother. They were tall, lean, ruddy-faced, and they were blonde, red-headed, or they had dark hair but nowhere as dark as mine. One of my fellow patients was there because of a broken leg from a jeep accident. Another had been operated on for appendicitis. Two had malaria, as I did, and we shared a special kinship. Every afternoon the three of us would tremble in our cots, freezing, asking for more blankets in the humid 90-degree heat and trying desperately to lock our jaws to keep our teeth from chattering. For most of my adult life, I have suffered from malaria symptoms. Until well into my fifties, I took to my bed in the late afternoon and endured the wracking chills and the raging fever that follows.

We spent six weeks in the Sixth Casualty Camp in Leyte waiting for a troopship with space to take us home. When I see reruns of the television show *M.A.S.H.*, I recognize the authenticity of the set—the mud, the mess tent, the incoming wounded and the movies at 1900 hours. We ate Spam and powdered eggs and the beverage known as "battery acid." For my family, it was as luxurious a stay as we could have wanted in a five-star hotel.

We were still in Leyte when the atom bomb was dropped on Hiroshima and then on Nagasaki. My parents and their friends discussed it in hushed tones, but its world-changing significance was lost on me. Two months before, when President Roosevelt died, my father worried aloud about what would happen now with an unknown vice-president in that seat of awesome responsibility.

The night of August 15 (west of the International Dateline) we were sitting on plank benches in an outdoor movie theater watching *The Great John L*. The film flickered, sputtered and died; the sound went off and the audience hissed and booed. It was not an infrequent occurrence. Movies in rest camps were not known for their trouble-free projection.

A voice came over the public address system: *"The Emperor of Japan has offered to surrender."*

There was an explosion of pandemonium. Within minutes, all the search-lights in the camp were turned on and rolled back and forth across the sky. Men were jumping up and down like children in pure joy. Sand and gravel trucks on their way to more airstrip construction squealed to a stop in the middle of the road by their Seabee drivers, who dumped their loads and abandoned the vehicles to join in the jubilation. Sirens were sounding, horns were blasting, every kind of noisemaker was added to the din.

My parents hustled us back to our tent and packed us into bed and then they went out to join in the revelry. I went to sleep in the early hours of the morning, listening to those in the tent next door, to the voices of wounded men who could not leave their beds to celebrate, singing.

There's a long, long trail a-winding . . . into the land of my dreams
Where the nightingale is singing and the white moon beams.
There's a long, long night of waiting until my dreams all come true. . . .
Till the day when I'll be going down that long, long trail with you.

Historian Ronald H. Spector, in his book, *The American War with Japan: Eagle against the Sun*, offers a quote that says it best. "For all the fake manliness of our facades, we cried with relief and joy," confided a twenty-one-year-old second lieutenant platoon leader. "We were going to live. We were going to grow up to adulthood after all."

The next day we boarded the troopship USS *General Brewster* to make the final journey to our home in the United States.

22

San Francisco

/ / /

The pier on the San Francisco waterfront on September 1, 1945, led us into an icy wind that swirled over gangplanks and railings, snapping flags atop the Ferry Building, stinging our faces and legs, making us hold our hands over our ears to protect them from the cold.

Beyond the waterfront, streamers of fog were blowing in from the Pacific Ocean on the other side of the city, like white curtains whipping out of an open window. It was the same Pacific Ocean I had played in most of my life.

The San Francisco temperature was the coldest my brother and I had ever known. We said nothing to each other as we walked the length of the gangplank, trailing behind our parents, from the USS *General Brewster* to the California shore. There were too many strange things for us to absorb on that September afternoon. Our senses were overwhelmed with unaccustomed sights, unaccustomed noises, unaccustomed smells, and unaccustomed impressions. I was both anxious and eager, and there was a big lump in my throat, a lump that took up all the air I would need if I tried to talk. I don't think anyone else in the small band of war refugees from the Philippines could speak. I recall the sight of the busy docks and the beautiful white city beyond that spread upward over the hills. I think now that those moments were muffled with emotion and no one around me made a coherent sound.

As soon as the *General Brewster* sailed under the Golden Gate Bridge into San Francisco Bay, the soldiers and sailors coming home broke into wild celebration. Many of them were crying. Most were leaping into the air and shouting with joy. Some were very still, numb, silent. We watched the fireboats circling our troopship, hoses spraying seawater jubilantly into the air. There were commercial tour boats and private yachts and Bay ferries loaded with people—American people—screaming "welcome home," as they sidled up as close as possible to our ship. There were brass bands on some of the boats and women dancing the cancan and the conga, kicking their legs high in chorus lines.

Japan had surrendered. World War II was nearly over. The final act in the war took place on September 2, our second day in the United States, exactly a month after my twelfth birthday, with the signing of a treaty of peace in Tokyo Bay.

The voyage from the Philippines to the United States took about sixteen days, as I recall. We traveled in a convoy of naval ships in slow zigzag formation. Even though hostilities were ended, theoretically, the U.S. Navy took no chances that some renegade Japanese submarine or kamikaze pilot hadn't gotten the word.

The *General Brewster* was a Coast Guard boat that had been commissioned to transport troops from Europe, where that part of the war had ended in June, to New Guinea to fight again in the Pacific. After off-loading in New Guinea, it proceeded to Leyte, where it picked up a boatload of soldiers, sailors, airmen, WACs and nurses rotating home, and about forty bedraggled repatriates.

My brother and I explored the ship as soon as we were underway at Tacloban. We tried to see every inch of it, although we were told there were some areas that were off-limits to everyone but the ship's crew. I think Jorge J. managed to make an exception of himself to that rule, because he told of a number of places on board where the delighted sailors welcomed a curious nine-year-old boy. They treated him as their own son or little brother.

We especially enjoyed going up and down the steep staircases in the ship, and there were a lot of them. There were several abandon-ship drills called during our voyage, which added excitement to the otherwise dull routine. When we were not asleep we had to wear life vests at all times. The vests weren't made for children and they were very heavy and very hot, so my brother and I were extremely uncomfortable, but we tried not to complain.

Mostly, we played out on the deck, where the homeward-bound GIs marveled that we could walk barefooted on the iron decking, which was like a broiler grill in the sun. I spent hours and hours reading, in what was probably the last period in my life when I had nothing else to do. Perhaps this would have been an opportune time for my mother to make me learn the multiplication tables. However, for whatever reason, she did not think to do that.

Miraculously, I didn't get seasick along the way. The ship was heavy enough and slow enough that the ocean waves didn't seem to affect it. We women repatriates and the nurses and WACs were quartered three bunks high in the officers' cabins above deck. My dad and my brother slept down in the hold, where the hammock-bunks were hung in stacks. Jorge J. said the vertical space between beds was barely enough for him to turn over, and he was a scrawny little kid. Imagine how claustrophobic that must have been for a grown man. But, like us, the troops didn't complain. They were just glad to be going home, no matter the discomfort.

The long sea journey was salubrious in effect, the ship serving as a kind of decompression chamber not only for the war-weary soldiers but also for the adult and child refugees. We enjoyed the navy's good food, we had showers, and we didn't have to walk anywhere. The USS *General Brewster* has held a warm place in my heart ever since. My daughter reminds me how I always pointed out the decommissioned naval fleet "moth-balled" in Suisun Bay on the Carquinez Straits northeast of San Francisco. She was born just a few miles from that spot, and we often drove to the city on I-680 while she was growing up. I didn't know, at that time, that the *General Brewster* was one of those ships.

"I think you always felt that your ship was there," my daughter said.

On the way to San Francisco from the Philippines, the only stop we made was at Honolulu. Two families among our fellow passengers were Hawaiian—and they were home. They disembarked but none of the rest of us could go ashore. However, the small boat that came out to take off the Hawaii passengers brought boxes of clothing gathered and packed by the Hawaii Red Cross, and we joyously went through the boxes, trying on, selecting skirts and pants, blouses and dresses, and shoes that fit, even marginally. I managed to get my feet in a pair of well-worn dirty white, open-toed shoes with wedge heels. They were not the most elegant shoes I would ever wear but I shall always be grateful to the girl who donated them so I could wear them when I went into The City.

Because the clothes were collected in Hawaii, there were no heavy coats or long-sleeved sweaters but we were just glad to have a change of clothing and we had no earthly idea how cold it would be in San Francisco.

My brother was not very lucky at finding shoes in the Honolulu gift box. There were none to fit a little boy. He did find a shirt and a pair of short pants just his size. Before we left Leyte, Mother had made him a khaki "overseas" cap like our father's, so he was almost natty, albeit barefooted.

Aunt Charlotte, I must add, was the best dressed of all the women, even as we left Leyte. She had the presence of mind to have a woolen olive-drab army blanket tailored into a double-breasted three-quarter-length coat with resplendent mother-of-pearl buttons, lined in white silk, made for her by the finest tailor in Bacolod. When Aunt Charlotte walked off the USS *General Brewster*, she looked like a million dollars—and she was the only one who was warm.

As we entered the wharfside building where we were to be processed into the United States, we were met by a contingent of Gray Ladies, Red Cross volunteers assigned to greet our refugee group. A beautiful woman with pale silver hair, wearing a silver-gray suit and pearl gray stockings and high-heeled gray leather opera pumps, and a gray wool cape bearing the Red Cross insignia on her shoulders, came to me and wrapped me in a patchwork woolen afghan.

The wool was scratchy but it immediately shut away the cold. I began to say, "Thank you," but the beautiful woman turned away, not knowing, I'm sure, that I could speak her language. I had met my first San Franciscan.

23

Oklahoma

/ / /

The last leg of our journey to our American home was on the Atchison, Topeka and Santa Fe train. We left San Francisco (actually Oakland) and traveled halfway across the United States to Woodward, which was on the Santa Fe line. The trip was a blur. I recall that we were in a Pullman car and we slept in beds that folded into the ceiling or into the seats. We crossed the Great American Desert and the Continental Divide and the plains of the Texas and Oklahoma panhandles. When we arrived in Woodward, there was truly a crowd at the train station and most of the people there were related to me.

My uncle Marshall and his family were there except for the two sons, Jack and Bill, who were still in the Pacific, and a daughter, Loydene, who was a WAC. My cousins Gracie and Maude Allen, the children of Aunt Frances, were there, except for John, who also was still in the army. My aunt Maude, my mother's beloved dearest sister, was there with her husband,

Uncle Bruce Vaughn, who later tried valiantly to make a pianist of me. (It was a futile effort. I just didn't have his talent.) Aunt Mattie was there with her teenage son, Dick. There were Pittman cousins who had grown up with Mother, and their children and grandchildren. There were Fourth Street neighbors of my late grandparents and fellow members of the First Christian Church. There was the reporter from the *Woodward Daily Press*.

After much hugging and kissing, we went directly to Aunt Mattie's house with most of the cousins and aunts and uncles, where I was presented a birthday cake with twelve candles and my name in red icing. We talked and ate, and ate and talked at Aunt Mattie's dining table. It was the precursor of many such family gatherings over the next decade.

I've spent a lifetime learning to appreciate how generous my father and mother's families were with each other. In the Philippines our Filipino relatives adored my mother. Of course, my memory of that devotion is most vivid from when I observed the cousins who were living in Northern California, and who became acquainted with us after the war. Likewise, never did any of my American aunts and uncles treat my father as anyone other than a member of the family. My dad genuinely loved his in-laws. My U.S. relatives saw him as a war hero and my mother's hometown friends reveled in his war stories.

Our Harrison relatives were beautifully warm and welcoming and loving. None of them treated us like strangers and to this day I can't thank them enough for their ready embrace. Even now, more than ever, I realize how valuable they were—and are—to our well-being. They just wouldn't let us feel left out, and still don't.

If anyone was uncomfortable with my biracial status, it was I. My brother didn't seem to know there was any difference between us and them. Mother took her place in the community with quiet grace, and Dad was a celebrity. I was the adolescent and perhaps I would have gone through that troubled phase of insecurity regardless of my heritage.

We hardly rested from our trip half around the world because there were things to be done. Jorge J. and I started school in Woodward, I think, the day following our arrival. Based on my mother's assessment, I went into the fifth grade and my brother was placed in second grade.

My dad's health was the primary issue. The inguinal hernia was at a critical stage. The next most important problem was a job, an income. Mother was the only potential wage earner and she started within hours to apply for a teaching job wherever there was a possibility. We lived for several weeks with Aunt Mattie in her two-bedroom house, and comfortable as it was for two people, it was definitely too small for four more. The house that my late grandparents left to my mother was occupied by renters and my parents didn't want to terminate the rental until Mother found work.

We still had some financial help from the Red Cross—I do believe Mother saved some of the original stipend we received in San Francisco— and whenever we were invited to events to tell about our experiences, a "love offering" was taken up to help us with expenses. I'm sure Mother gave whatever was available to Aunt Mattie for our room and board. I don't remember buying clothes or sodas or going to movies unless Uncle Bruce took us.

In October, Mother was hired to teach in the high school at Logan, New Mexico. Dad had abdominal surgery in the Veterans' Hospital in Amarillo, Texas. It was another of those propitious happenings that we attribute to the ever-living and ever-loving God. Logan was a not-too-long Greyhound bus ride from Amarillo, so Mother was able to be with Daddy every weekend while he was recovering. Jorge J. and I were old enough, responsible enough certainly, to take care of ourselves in Logan while Mother was at the hospital with Dad.

In the eight months that I attended Logan fifth grade, I learned what it was to be nonwhite. A substantial percentage of the Logan students were

Native Americans. Some were a mixture of Hispanic and Navajo, or Hispanic and Apache. The Anglo students, the "whites," ignored their darker-skinned, dark-haired, dark-eyed classmates. I was not accustomed to being ignored nor willing to be snubbed. Most of the Anglo kids were the children of ranchers, not necessarily culturally advanced but superior nonetheless for their "whiteness," which they seemed to equate with being American.

I was caught in between. I looked Apache, Navajo, or Hispanic, but I spoke better English than any of the Anglos. I had one or two Anglo friends who liked me. The Native Americans would have nothing to do with me, probably because I was so uppity. The rest of the students either bullied me or looked right through me. I can't remember which was worse.

It wasn't easy, living in New Mexico with our dad in the Veterans' Hospital in Amarillo. And anyone who has weathered an eastern New Mexico winter will understand what a test of fortitude it was for my brother and me, who never before experienced a temperature below freezing. When May came, Mother was told there was a teaching vacancy in Woodward the following school year and she got the job. Dad was discharged from the Veterans' Hospital and the U.S. Army. We moved back to Woodward and into my grandparents' house on Fourth Street—and we were finally, truly, at home. It was home for our family during the next twelve years.

24

"What Was the War Really Like?"

/ / /

"What did you do in the jungle while you were hiding out from the Japanese?"

"What did you eat? What did you wear? Were you afraid of wild animals? Were there lots of snakes?"

"Did you have playmates? Where did you go to school?"

"Did you see a lot of dead bodies?"

Those were the questions my brother and I were asked after the war. We answered them the best we could but, to this day, I don't think we could ever have verbalized what the war was *really* like. There isn't a way to describe a life-endangering, life-changing experience to someone else, particularly someone whose concept of danger was perhaps limited to fear of the dark and for whom deprivation meant going without ice cream because of sugar rationing.

I am reminded of the Edgar Lee Masters poem, "Silence," in which a veteran of the Civil War is asked by a young boy, "How did you lose your leg?" and the old soldier replies, "A bear bit it off." I first read Masters' poetry when I was nine years old and I didn't know that only a few years later, I would understand full well how the Civil War survivor could not bring himself to tell about the horror of Gettysburg.

Neither Jorge J. nor I could envision fear of the dark or feeling deprived because of a sugar shortage, so we had no words to convey how we coped with the dangers we experienced from 1941 to 1945. When we first came to the U.S. we were asked to make public appearances to talk about our war experiences, and so we would rise to the occasion and make a more or less standard speech to a roomful of people. That wasn't hard, but generally it was our dad who did most of the public speaking—he was good at it, despite his broken English, and he liked doing it.

Were we frightened during the war? Sometimes yes, but most of the time we were buoyed in our certainty that Mom and Dad would keep us safe. We were not unknowing about the dangers we faced, and we were rarely lied to by our parents about the gravity of our situation. At the same time, they instilled in us confidence that all four of us had the will and the know-how to stay alive.

I recall, in 1940, my parents' friend, Anne Merado, quoting a radio newscast she had just heard that American forces could annihilate the Japanese within seventy-two hours. It was mentioned during a rare trip north for my brother and me, when we stayed the night with friends. After dinner, my parents and their hosts were lingering over glasses of dessert wine. I was put to bed, where I listened to every word they said and marked it down in my memory. Eighteen months later, Anne Merado was in Santo Tomas concentration camp and I was safe in far southern Negros Island.

My father and mother did not underestimate the Japanese; both of them had seen the efficiency and ambition of Japanese immigrants. Yet they too were lulled by faith that the United States would come to the aid of American soldiers and sailors trapped in Asia, and of Filipinos who were America's staunchest ally in the Pacific. Nonetheless, our mother and father calmly schooled us in survivor behavior when and if the enemy confronted us.

"When you hear airplanes, you kids get under cover and don't come out until I come and get you." My mother's cautionary words were never any more dramatic than that. If we asked her what would happen when the Japanese came, I recall she said simply, "They're not going to find us here, kiddies. We'll be off in the mountains and they won't want to come looking for us up there."

I believe my parents rehearsed these responses with each other so much that they had convinced themselves as well as Jorge J. and me that we were safe and far away from the cities and towns where the enemy was a real threat.

My brother and I were shielded from the reports of guerrilleros and village folk concerning acts of Japanese atrocities in Luzon and other islands closer by, but we couldn't help hearing tag-ends of conversations and reading the faces of those who told our parents of the fearful happenings. I don't remember even knowing about the Bata-an death march and the fall of Corregidor—to a child of nine, what went on in other parts of the country was of small import, even though our father had gone off to fight the Japanese and our mother rationed whatever milk we had with lunch. In 1942 there wasn't any television or radio that could bring us all the horrible news of the day. Our Manila newspaper was no longer delivered. Even the vaunted bamboo telegraph, that most original of communication systems, did not touch my brother and me, though we exchanged information with each other and tried to understand the danger we were in by the war.

I don't think our parents intentionally kept us ignorant about what could happen when and if the Japanese found us. They were matter-of-fact about our situation and managed to convey to us, six- and nine-year-old children, in a calm way, that we had to take responsibility for our safety, even as they would see to it that we would be safe.

After we left our house on the beach to live at the edge of the mountains and the jungle, Jorge J. and I rarely had friends of our own age to play with. My father was adamant that the fewer people who knew where we were, the safer we would be. While we heard that virtual colonies of American families huddled together in wartime hideouts on the island, my parents felt more secure to go it alone. We had one or two young guerrilleros with us at all times, mostly to serve as sentries and to carry sacks of rice and other necessities when we were on the move, but Dad knew that people could be bribed or threatened into betrayal, and although he trusted his countrymen, he understood what torture and terror could do. Hence, we were the loners of Negros Island.

The history and horror of war are most often described in terms of the combatants, I think. Much has been written about the bravery, the hardships endured by American soldiers, and I grant you, nothing can be said that could possibly diminish their heroism in every battle they have ever fought.

When I am asked what it was like to survive a war, I can only speak as a child who was there. However proud I am of my father's leadership, his service as a U.S. Army officer before the Philippines surrender and then in the guerrilla movement, his devotion to my mother and my brother and me, I have to include tragic things that happened to civilians trying to go about their ordinary business during that war.

When I was not yet ten years old, I heard a story that even today is painful for me to recall. Farmers often caught fish that were somewhat like our mudcat, in the rice paddies while the fields were flooded after planting. One evening, a man stopped on his way home hoping to catch a nice catfish or two for the family dinner. Somehow, the first fish he caught jumped into the man's mouth and became lodged in his throat. Neighbors nearby came to rescue him but couldn't pull the fish out.

The guerrillero relating this story said, "They tried to pull out the fish with pliers, but the more they pulled, the deeper the fins of the fish caught in his throat." The man soon died for lack of oxygen.

My brother, on reading the manuscript of this book recently, corrected my long-held impression of how the fish got into the man's throat.

"He was noodling," my brother said. "He'd caught that first fish and stuck it between his teeth, and was going after another one when he accidently swallowed his catch."

Noodling? I learned about "noodling" only recently when I read a newspaper article about the fishing sport that is popular with many Oklahomans.

"I hear guys talk about going noodling and I always think of that poor fellow who died with the fish in his throat," my brother said.

The most dangerous wild animals in the jungle were the feral pigs that nested among the rocks where we set up our evacuation camps. Wild boar was sought-after game before the war and certainly during the war when meat was hard to come by. It was not unusual for us to buy wild pig meat from hunters while we lived in Cartagena. It's hard to imagine a pig as a dangerous animal (unless you've been around even the domesticated variety), but there is no more ferocious creature than a sow protecting her young. I once saw a man who had been mauled by a wild pig. He came to our house seeking treatment for his injuries and my father and mother did what they could to save the man's life, but without the ability to suture his wounds, stanch his bleeding, replace his blood loss and relieve his pain, their efforts were futile. He died of shock and infection within days.

When we went into the mountains in the latter half of 1942, we took our dogs Buster and Wainwright. They were good company and we still had enough scraps from our meals to feed them. Mother thought they served a good purpose as watchdogs. One afternoon, during which my brother and I were ostensibly "in school," we heard a terrible ruckus out in the jungle. The dogs were growling and barking and we could hear them raising Cain among the banyan trees and the clumps of giant fern. Mother grabbed her biggest bolo and ran down the path to see what Buster and Wainwright were so upset about. My brother and I followed.

The two dogs had a huge monitor lizard between them. Buster had the monster by the head, and Wainwright's jaws were clamped on the lizard's tail. The two dogs were playing tug-of-war with the unfortunate reptile. My mother whacked the bolo through the lizard's middle and separated the dogs from their victim. When laid out and measured, the creature was more than four feet long.

But the monitor lizard wasn't a danger to us. Nor were the wild macaws and the monkeys. There were snakes, but I never saw one. Actually, wild creatures were the guardians of the jungle. Birds and reptiles and small mammals sounded the alarm when something unnatural was in the area, and I have no doubt snakes played their role in the biological security system as well.

25

Now I Know My Father

* / / /*

Like combat veterans of every war, Dad drifted emotionally for a year or two after he was discharged from the army. He was still recuperating from major surgery and it was hard on him for people to know how physically restricted he was. The depression that he suffered was devastating and it took every ounce of my mother's love to bring him through that painful period of adjustment. Even the terror in the mountains of Negros had been perhaps less debilitating than the current sense of helplessness caused by his physical condition and the uselessness he felt in a country that was not yet his own. Mother was the breadwinner—and Dad's traditional masculine role cried out against that anomaly. As a teacher, Mother did not command a handsome salary, so we were on a very strict budget. I don't know what veterans' benefits if any, besides the hospitalization, my dad was allowed. In years to come, my parents valiantly petitioned for Dad's U.S. Army back pay because he had fought as a United States Army officer from 1941 to 1945, four years, without salary or benefits. Despite his friends in Congress and other high places, Dad's pleas were denied. The only concession the Department of Defense made to my father's noble World War II service was a military funeral and a soldier's headstone in Tulsa's Memorial Cemetery. My mother was never accorded widow's benefits or recognition as the wife of a soldier in the U.S. Army.

Late in 1946, Dad was contacted by old friends at Oklahoma A&M College who helped him get a job as a technical assistant in the United Nations Relief and Recovery Administration. He was sent to China, to Hunan province, where he spent two years providing agricultural information and assistance to Chinese farmers. Dad learned to speak both the Mandarin and the Cantonese languages while he was on that assignment. When he came home in mid-1949, Dad brought three trunkloads of gifts. They included bolts of silk, embroidered wall hangings, beautiful porcelains, and carved artwork. Many of these treasures now are displayed in my home and it thrills me to see them, especially when I am quietly drinking my early morning coffee in my dining room.

Dad completed a master's degree in agriculture economics at A&M after his China tour. He wrote his thesis on the soil conservation movement in Oklahoma, of all things, and for one summer he was an unpaid intern at the U.S. Department of Agriculture / Oklahoma A&M Experimental Field Station in Woodward. He became a lifelong friend of the young station superintendent, Pat McIlvain. Now I walk an hour every day that I can through what is formally named the Southern Plains Range Research Station. I think about my dad on those walks, recalling how he enjoyed the trees and wildlife that I'm sure made him homesick for the Philippines.

After the Mao Tse Tung Communist takeover in 1949, UNRRA was discontinued in China. Another career door opened in my father's life, one more fulfilling than ever. President Truman appointed Dr. Henry G. Bennett, president of Oklahoma A&M, head of the Point Four Program, an international consortium proposed by President Roosevelt in his 1943 postwar recovery plan. Dr. Bennett picked my father to be among the original team members to implement Point Four, and he worked under the auspices of the U.S. Department of State from 1950 to 1963. He was assigned to Indonesia for six years, where he learned to speak the language of Sumatra and acquired a working knowledge of Dutch. He worked in the Medan and Djakarta areas, developing better agricultural practices.

Mother remained in Woodward until my brother graduated from high school and I from college. She retired from teaching in 1956, sold their home, and for the second time, crossed the Pacific going west, this time in an airliner, to join my father. Now they would be together until he died of prostate cancer in December of 1963.

In addition to his assignment in Indonesia, Dad was sent to Cuba, British Guiana, and Chile. In each of those countries, he polished up his Spanish, but he was always scornful of the regional misuse of his favorite language. He was as picky about Hispanic grammar and pronunciation as I am about incorrect English.

The Four Point program was renamed the Agency for International Development (USAID) and has since been privatized and operated by corporate contractors. My father was very proud to be a member of "The Hunger Fighters," as his group was called. Many of his fellow workers were Oklahoma A&M alumni, so he was very much at home.

Had he lived to enjoy his retirement, my father would have spent his leisure years visiting friends all over the United States and throughout the world. He kept up with his colleagues by letters and phone calls whenever he was in their vicinity. After he died, I urged Mother to stay in contact with his cronies, to continue the friendships he had established over the years. Mother began to weep when I suggested that she travel and I was impatient with her lack of motivation. Now I know, now I finally understand, what partners they were, how each of them nurtured the other for thirty-six years. For more than ten of those years, they lived apart, on opposite sides of the earth, but when they returned to each other it was as if Dad had only been away on a short business trip. Their life together took up where it had left off, without missing a beat.

Theirs was not an egalitarian marriage as we might view it in the twenty-first century. Except for the lunches my father prepared when he was at home, Mother did all the housework, in addition to her demanding career as a teacher. She took care of all of the family's business decisions, the bill-paying, the household repairs, the transportation. Dad was never comfortable driving a car, although he had an Oklahoma driver's license. He never got over his disinterest in things mechanical, and I suffer from the same handicap. When we owned a car in the Philippines, before we went to live beyond the highway, we had a chauffeur.

Both my father and mother, however, loved to cook—and that's a skill my brother and I very proudly inherited. When he was at home between assignments, Dad made lunch for us if it was during the school year, and the lunch was always the same—a delectable soup using chicken and many kinds of vegetables with soy sauce and lots of garlic over rice. Only his granddaughter Sara can duplicate that flavor and I think her ability is decidedly genetic because none of us ever wrote down my father's recipe. If he was on home leave during the summer, Dad was in charge of the ornamental plants and flowers around our house. Mother's forte was the kitchen garden and the fruit trees that my grandfather had planted in our yard in the 1920s.

Before Dad left for his overseas career, his daughter was increasingly rebellious and self-righteous. I made myself the antithesis of what a Filipina daughter should be. The values he demonstrated were, in my mind, outdated, dismally conservative, out of touch with the hip (or, in those days, the hep) and the enlightened. Before I was thirteen, I cut off my long black braids, and I could never find the time nor energy to practice on the piano, although my parents spent good money for my instruction. I kept my friends away from the house when Dad was home because he embarrassed me and, besides, we lived in an old-fashioned grandma-grandpa neighborhood. I nagged Mom to build or buy a new brick ranch-style home in a newer part of town. She just looked at me incredulously. Even though my father had a fairly high Civil Service rating with a decent salary, that plus her $300 or $400-a-month teaching salary was hardly enough to pay cash for a new brick home. And cash was the only way they ever purchased anything. Besides, every penny not spent on basic living expenses went into the college fund they were saving for Jorge J. and me, a fund that they astonishingly accumulated in less than five years.

Worst of all, I rarely spoke directly to my father or made eye contact. When he asked me questions, I responded with muttered monosyllables. Now I know what he wanted of me—simple courtesy, pleasant manners, and above all, filial respect and consideration and esteem—virtues that I identified with being Filipina. It didn't occur to me that those were the same virtues that were expected of my friends by their parents. As far as I was concerned, my father was invisible.

Then Jorge Arzaga Madamba discovered there were those who truly needed him—the hungry, the illiterate, and the deprived. Not unacquainted with the poor and the downtrodden, he found a way to serve them. Through the United Nations, the Point Four program, and the Agency for International Development, my father used his knowledge and vitality to ease their poverty by teaching them modern ways to grow food. He brought them a tiny few steps into the world of technology and abundance—and he alleviated some of their deprivation.

When he was almost fifty years old, my father began a whole new career and, for the next fifteen years, he worked to help the illiterate, the malnourished, the poorest of the poor, the put-down, by-passed, mistreated people of five different countries, where political indifference, social injustice, and poor health kept them captive. My dad was a one-man middle-aged Peace Corps before the Peace Corps was founded. What he did probably made not a jot's difference in the cauldron of human suffering but he did it because he was needed. He never returned to live in the Philippines, although several times he passed through Manila on his way to somewhere else in Asia, making quick visits to the surviving members of his family and I'm sure giving them lavish gifts he could ill afford.

In 1956, Jorge J. started to college. I was married and my first child, Jayne, was born just before Mother left the States. For the next seven years, my parents were always together, except when she managed to come back to Oklahoma for a few weeks for the birth of my son Kevin and my husband's graduation from the University of Oklahoma School of Medicine.

For all these years since World War II, I sidestepped my father's place in my identity. I didn't want to understand him, didn't want to let him be a part of my life. I wanted to put him away like the memory of the humid, dark jungle, the strange and dangerous life we lived there, and the complicated non-Indo-European language that my brother and I learned to speak as toddlers.

Some years ago, a friend casually told me of a remark made by a woman who had gone to college with my father. "He was the most intelligent man I've ever known," the woman said.

That comment was the real catalyst for this memoir. I resolved to look at Dad as he truly was. Therein I found the most singular characteristic of my father to which I am drawn, of which I am most proud: his intelligence, which I had refused to recognize.

My father, Jorge Arzaga Madamba, was diligent, honest, resolute, and steadfast. He was kind and loving and cheerful and strong. But it was his intelligence that made him more than just the sum of all those parts. He was a man more splendid for using his mind.

Epilogue
This Side of the Looking Glass

///

It would be two decades before I allowed myself to think about the war and its effect on me. During the intervening years I struggled in a solitary conflict of my own. From 1945 until 1963, all my energy was devoted to blending into the America where I wanted my life to be free of the war and my Filipina heritage. If the subject of my childhood in the Philippines surfaced, I dismissed it as if that experience were nothing more than a random occurrence, insignificant, unimportant. I discarded it.

One day in 1965, two years after my father died, I had to confront that war with all its pain and all its brutality. My husband and I were driving home to Oroville, the small Northern California town where we lived. We were returning from a leisurely, luxurious weekend in San Francisco. I read the Sunday *San Francisco Chronicle* as my husband drove. In the magazine section was a piece written by a man describing the return of his only son in a body bag from Vietnam. It was a simple story. I read it out loud to my husband and as we traveled through the green farmland of the Sacramento Valley, I began to cry.

The young man's death was far removed from me. I was a thirty-two-year-old housewife, the mother of four children. The politics of Communism and Southeast Asia and the United States were vague, muddled, masked in confusion in my mind. But the newspaper story took me back to the years I'd spent as a child in a war—and I began to grieve, for myself and then for all of humankind.

The years that separated me from a day in 1945 when I walked down a gangplank from the USS *General Brewster* to a San Francisco pier were a bridge back to my real identity. I wept for the child that I was who lived through a war, for the family that struggled so desperately to stay alive, and then for my own little children, my two-year-old and eight-year-old sons, my five-year-old and ten-year-old daughters.

I wept for the Japanese pilot shot dead in the sea, for Father Oomun sending his message for help on a ham radio, for Colonel Neil Britain disappeared forever in a sinking hell ship, and for Crispin the guerrillero who endured a ruptured stomach and punctured lungs and a fractured skull at the hands of his Japanese captors to buy time for my mother and my brother and me to escape into a wild pig cave.

I wept for Robert Howard's fine clean name stenciled in black on a white wooden cross with his dog tags draped upon it, leaning against a Quonset hut wall, waiting for the graves detail to implant it on a Negros Island hillside where crosses marched into the Pacific horizon.

Most of all, for the first time, I wept for my father who died one month after John Kennedy died, another survivor of that cruel war. I wept because I never fully comprehended how they virtually sacrificed their lives for me. And never before had I wept for the loss of my father.

Now my generation was undertaking the same sacrifice.

"Why?" I said to my husband. "Why are we doing this? What will be accomplished by the killing of young men and children, and women young and old? Will we prove anything? Will this killing solve anything?"

"We have to win this war," my husband said. "We are in a fight-to-the-death conflict with the Communists. If we don't prevail in Vietnam, they will prevail over us. It's a matter of pride. It's a matter of honor."

I wondered how pride and honor comforted the man whose son's body was coming in on a Blue Canoe at Travis Air Force Base.

I could not stop weeping. The miles went by as we drove home through the tomato fields, the rice lands, the peach orchards, the almond and walnut and mandarin groves. The great valley oaks of Northern California, rising into the sky and sweeping low to the ground, denizens of hundreds of years in this glorious state, this glorious land, made me remember the Philippine jungle.

All of the chauvinism that I had so carefully nurtured for twenty years became a veil of sadness. Through that veil I saw that to be an American did not mean being oblivious to the terrible consequences of war, defining enemies and satisfying hate by killing people and thence killing ourselves. For the first time since that September day in 1945 when a treaty of peace was signed in Tokyo Bay while a council known as the United Nations met in the San Francisco War Memorial Opera House, as I left behind me my childhood in the Philippines and walked ashore in California finally an American, I confronted in my mind the uselessness of shooting and blowing up and bombing and mauling other human beings, the futility of reprisal, the cruelty of fear, and the horror of hunger and pain.

In Vietnam it was happening all over again.

I wanted to tell my husband that war is a personal tragedy, not a policy decision nor a strategic move to attain a political goal. I wanted him to feel the fear and the deprivation, the longing for safety and plentiful food and being able to sing aloud and wear something nicer than ragged clothes four years too small. I wish I could have told him what it was to have spent three years memorizing four or five books by reading them over and over again, and wishing I could go to a school with classmates and real classrooms. I couldn't begin to describe what it was like not to have a toilet or toilet paper, or a toothbrush or a fork, a table and a china plate, or a lamp of any kind.

War as I knew it was a personal tragedy not just for me but for every other human being in the world. I wanted my husband to know that war is not justified by national pride or economic expedience or one group's best interests versus another's, and that it is not absolved by religious certainties or political theory or social dogma. I wanted him to know that war is the hurting of children, the killing of strong men and women, the suffering of old people. I wanted to say that for those who send their young to die, the pain is more than the human spirit can bear.

I tried to speak to my husband about it and he said harshly, "Whose side are you on anyway?"

I shook my head as tears washed down my face. I couldn't answer.

As I write this, it is more than fifty years after the end of World War II. My early life has become an abstraction. I was born in a far foreign land to unconventional parentage and I was reared with people who were a melange of Malaysian, Melanesian, Oriental, European, Spanish and American. When I learned to talk, I spoke in two languages simultaneously and interchangeably. But the moment I stepped foot on United States soil, I never again uttered a Visayan sentence. I purposefully and completely lost the ability to communicate in a Filipino language.

On that island in the Pacific where I spent my early childhood it was western Oklahoma that shaped my personality and molded my mind. The stolid Kansans and immigrant Germans of Ellis County, my mother's people, stood over me, invisible but stern, judging my thoughts, calling to account my actions. Blended into my upbringing were the epic idylls of Tennyson and the genius writings of Mark Twain. Those cultures influenced me while I existed in a vacuum. It was all I had during the war.

My life is a study in paradox. I have been endangered and protected and I have been privileged and deprived. I can sing a hundred hymns without a hymnal and I've read much of the Bible, but I question Christianity because it has been so twisted and revised and used as an alibi for war that it seems to have lost the voice of Jesus. The simple food I ate in my childhood was from the earth and from the sea. Now it is expensive and sophisticated and I savor it more than any other.

I have lived in shacks of nipa and slept on floors of split bamboo, but I have also lived in a beautiful house with white carpeting and a grand piano. I treasure a tea service of sterling silver and wine glasses of Austrian crystal but for four years in my childhood I ate from a scooped-out coconut shell and drank clear water with my cupped hand from a jungle spring.

In 1945 a San Francisco lady wrapped me in a woolen afghan to warm me from the cold, but she turned away before I could say, "Thank you," because she didn't know I could speak her language. If we knew each other today, we would sit together at my dinner table and we might discuss the ballet.

Throughout my life I've known suspicion and fear, betrayal and rage, and hate and brutality, but I believe in tolerance and gentleness and love. I have been called too trusting. I have many friends, and yet I am lonely. I belong to a warm family and I have reared four fine children, but all of them are now far from me. I would like to live in many places on the earth—the south of France; northern Japan; Monterey Bay and Eureka,

California; and the Mexican city of Oaxaca—but the place I call home is a small town in northwest Oklahoma.

I am philosophically, emotionally, spiritually, and intellectually liberal but I live by rigid principles. I accept people for what they are, but I reject them for what they are not. I am patient with human flaws, but I am judgmental of human shortcomings. I have been loved as few have been loved, but at times I feel that I'm not loved enough.

My first marriage collapsed during the Vietnam War, but at the age of forty-four, I recovered and rebuilt my life, even as my mother did after the terror of World War II when she was exactly that age.

Widowed in 1963, Mother lived alone in Tulsa until she died of colon cancer in 1969. She loved the little house she and Daddy had designed for their retirement. It was all brick with cream-colored carpeting and tile in the kitchen, bathrooms, and laundry. All the appliances that my mother did without throughout her lifetime were finally hers—a washer and dryer, a dishwasher and garbage disposer, plenty of hot running water, automatically controlled central heating and air-conditioning, a car all her own, and a front lawn and backyard that she doted on.

Mother remained strong, physically and emotionally, until her death. One of her proudest accomplishments was when she was made chairman of the kitchen renovation committee of her church. She reveled in the purchasing of a commercial-size stove and refrigerator. She designed the cabinetry and counter tops for the best use of space, energy, and workflow. She picked out paint colors and building materials that were "practical." She was in her element.

Once or twice a year, she would come to California to see us and she usually stayed a month. While she was there she did a lot of baby-sitting and she left an impression on her grandchildren that I recognize and appreciate to this day.

Not long ago, my eldest son, Kevin, who is in his mid-forties, said of his grandmother Madamba, "She was the strongest woman I've ever known."

But I knew the soft side of my mother. She was giddy with pride in her children. A friend of mine who was in her classes in high school told me, "She talked about you all the time. After you went to college, we heard all about how you made the Dean's List for your grades, how you were chairman of this and that in student government. She showed us the evening gowns she was working on for you to wear to the fraternity balls, she brought in clippings of your news stories and your columns in the college newspaper." I was embarrassed to hear all this fifty years later, but I am happy that I made my mother proud.

After raising my own family and following a successful career, I feel sure that my father would be proud too. Now I say, with equal pride, "Thank you, Dad."